D1374176

BARRIERS TO ECUMENISM

BARRIERS TO ECUMENISM

*The Holy See and
the World Council of Churches
on Social Questions*

Thomas Sieger Derr

OCEAN COUNTY
COLLEGE LIBRARY
TOMS RIVER, N.J.
APR 1984
RECEIVED

ORBIS BOOKS
Maryknoll, New York 10545

261.83
D 438b

The Catholic Foreign Mission Society of America (Maryknoll) recruits and trains people for overseas missionary service. Through Orbis Books Maryknoll aims to foster the international dialogue that is essential to mission. The books published, however, reflect the opinions of their authors and are not meant to represent the official position of the society.

Copyright © 1983 by Orbis Books, Maryknoll, NY 10545
Manufactured in the United States of America
All rights reserved

Manuscript editor: Robert Cunningham

Library of Congress Cataloging in Publication Data

Derr, Thomas Sieger, 1931–
    Barriers to ecumenism.

    Includes bibliographical references and index.
    1. Church and social problems—Catholic Church.
2. Christian union—Catholic Church. I. Title.
HN37.C3D446   1983   261.8'3   82-18761
ISBN 0-88344-031-8 (pbk.)

CONTENTS

098889

788800

PREFACE

In 1978 I was asked to prepare a study that would serve as the major paper for the 1979 annual meeting of the Joint Working Group of the Roman Catholic Church and the World Council of Churches. The meeting that year was to be devoted to the question of common social witness. From the beginning it was understood to be an exercise with an unsettling purpose, namely, to say politely but frankly that cooperation between the two bodies was not working and to unearth the reasons. The paper was to be a catalyst that would force the issue and put an end to pretenses.

To this end the sponsors of the project gave me access to the people and materials I would need and turned me loose to discover and write what I would. As a "friendly outsider" not employed by either side but feeling a personal commitment to effective ecumenism, I began my task with hope and purposiveness. Naturally I set about reading the great heaps of documents cited in the notes of this book: mainly the highest level "official" statements of both organizations, including those issued by the assemblies and Central and Executive Committees of the WCC as well as by the popes and other top-level Vatican sources. But equally important, I also interviewed over twenty people in Rome and Geneva whose positions and experience gave them knowledge of and insight into my problem. Abetted by my promises of eternal confidentiality, and inspired as I was by the seriousness and promise of the task, they proved remarkably frank and rewarded me with candid appraisals of the difficulties as they saw them.

My synthesis and evaluation of these oral and written materials are presented here in considerably expanded and updated form. The original report, which was half as long as the present book, was duly delivered to the Joint Working Group in 1979, an audience I would characterize as attentive, involved, and nervous. Although the paper did not—and does not now—criticize any personalities, there were inevitably some who heard it that way; so there were, regrettably, some bruised feelings. Tension was also apparently caused by the simple candor of my remarks. The reader, I suspect, will find my formulations polite enough. They sounded rather different, however, to a group used to speaking in carefully wrought diplomatic niceties and in an atmosphere where to call an utterance "carefully nuanced" was high praise indeed.

When I finished speaking, the meeting adjourned uneasily to await discussion the next day. "Tomorrow," said one wise official to me privately, "they will kill your paper—but then they will eat the meat." In truth, something like that happened. There were plenty of defensive remarks, and people wondered aloud why I had to stir up difficulties. I replied simply that the problems were there, that I had not invented them, that they were felt keenly by responsible staff on both sides, and that they were not likely to go away soon. It was better to face the difficulties and see what sort of ecumenical cooperation could be managed under the circumstances.

The group then spent a couple of days working out a statement of future direction that, in fact, drew heavily on my outline of the problems. What one Vatican delegate called, I think appreciatively, my "well-organized frankness" passed into the next stage of ecumenical work. The following year, 1980, a new form of collaboration on social questions was established by the Joint Working Group, whose description was again strongly reminiscent of my original paper. This form, in turn, evolved into a new Joint

Consultative Group on Social Thought and Action in 1981. In short, this paper seems to have accomplished a good bit of what it was intended to do. Ecumenical work "at the summit" on social questions has at least been freshened. It is too soon to say more. The sequel will be written by the Holy See and the World Council in their own way—in response to history and to their own natures.

Meanwhile there is, I hope, some merit in offering the original paper to the public, though it has had to be updated to cover the last several years. It is helpful if all who hope in ecumenism understand the larger forces at work. The difficulties are not just a matter of a "conservative" Holy See facing a "radical" WCC, but of barriers arising out of their essential natures. Nothing will or can change quickly, but understanding is a step along the way.

Introduction

ECUMENICAL DECLINE

Most people who read this book will remember the ecumenical euphoria of the late sixties. It was the aftermath of the Second Vatican Council, which, it was said, signalled the formal entry of Rome into the ecumenical movement.[1] Structures were created to take advantage of the momentum. The Pontifical Commission Justice and Peace was founded in 1967 with the express intention of collaborating with the World Council of Churches. A Joint Working Group was established as a formal vehicle of cooperation between the WCC and the Roman Catholic Church; and in 1968 the two parent bodies created the Society for Development and Peace (Sodepax). Beyond collaboration, Roman Catholic membership in the WCC was openly discussed and by many both eagerly desired and confidently expected. The Uppsala Assembly of the WCC, in 1968, in approving the creation of the Joint Working Group noted "that former hesitations concerning the possibility of early understanding and cooperation have proved groundless" and urged attention to, and expressed its hope for, Catholic membership in the WCC.[2] The subject was formally considered by the Joint Working Group and by the Vatican Secretariat for Christian Unity in 1969 and 1970.[3] The high water mark of this positive phase, at least symbolically, was the visit of Pope Paul VI to the WCC in Geneva in June of 1969, a visit that seemed to seal the Roman Catholic commitment to genuine ecumenical cooperation.

But hopes had been raised too high and were soon disappointed. No doubt they were unrealistic from the beginning, certainly so in regard to the membership question. Pope Paul on his visit to Geneva called that a matter "not yet mature" which had a "long and difficult way to go"— sentiments echoed in slightly less pessimistic wording by Father Jerome Hamer of the Secretariat for Christian Unity.[4] But much more than membership was in trouble. The papal visit, itself clouded by ambiguity (against his will Paul was maneuvered into going by adroit staff work on both sides), may be read as a sign of the difficulties as much as of the hopes of ecumenism. Though Pope Paul spoke of the need for the "coordination of our efforts for social and economic development and for peace among the nations,"[5] the World Council had already found common social witness with the Vatican difficult.[6] The difficulty was to become more apparent in short order, and by 1970 or 1971, to use the blunt phrase of one of my informants, "the curtain fell." Not only was Roman Catholic membership out of the question but the Holy See was also reluctant to continue cooperative relations in critical areas, even delaying the renewal of Sodepax's mandate.[7]

The picture is, of course, more complex than these generalizations suggest. Sodepax did continue for a decade, albeit precariously, before finally succumbing in 1980, when it was allowed to die without any visible replacement for its functions. Catholics were, and are, members of the Faith and Order Commission and active participants in other World Council groups, studies, and conferences on evangelism and proselytism, medicine, dialogue with other faiths, international aid, and more. Five World Council staff attended the Synod of Bishops in 1971, and in 1975 the WCC and the Roman Catholic Church jointly sponsored a consultation on laity formation. Out on the field cooperative ventures grew apace. Cooperation, then, did not die aborning, but it was largely decentralized.

At the center, meanwhile, the tentative halfway measures of the early seventies were, as often happens to "temporary" arrangements, virtually institutionalized. The Joint Working Group has been renewed at regular intervals, becoming a substitute for Catholic membership in the WCC, quite against the intention of most of its creators. The Vatican seems to have settled quite contentedly for this anomalous situation, which enables the popes and other representatives to talk in general terms of the need to further Christian unity while avoiding concrete steps toward that unity which the Holy See does not wish to take. The formal, verbal commitment to ecumenism is still vigorous, the not-to-be-repudiated heritage of the Second Vatican Council. Rejecting any suggestion that ecumenism is floundering, or that it is dangerous or confusing, the bishops, Pope Paul, and especially Pope John Paul II have called the reunion of Christians a matter divinely willed. Like the older ecumenical movement represented by the World Council, they find the search for unity mandated by Christ himself in his prayer that his disciples might be one.[8]

But if active ecumenism is a duty of the faith, its terms tend to be defined in ways that make its realization unlikely. Anxious to appear (and to be) staunch defenders of the traditional faith in troubled times, the popes have repeatedly stressed that the purity of Catholic doctrine as defined by the historic teaching authority of the Church must be maintained without compromise in all ecumenical dialogue. Ecumenism can "in no way . . . mean giving up or in any way diminishing the treasures of divine truth that the church has constantly confessed and taught." These men give the impression that Christian unity resides in the charism of the papal office, and that reunion of the separated brethren with Rome is the desired conclusion of the process; for "the fullness of the revealed truths and of the means of salvation instituted by Christ is found in the Catholic Church."[9]

Accompanying this reassertion of Roman self-sufficiency is a renewed effort at central discipline within the Church that has had deleterious effects on the ecumenical movement. Catholics engaged in ecumenical relations have been cautioned to avoid "excessive zeal," and intercommunion is expressly forbidden. Limits on the forms for mixed marriages and the upbringing of their children continue to be unsatisfactory to non-Catholics. Catholic theologians, who have often been dramatically creative in ecumenical dialogue, have been warned and in some cases disciplined by Rome, reminded that they must stay within boundaries defined by the central authority:

> True freedom in teaching is necessarily contained within the limits of God's word, as this is constantly taught by the church's magisterium; likewise true freedom in research is necessarily based upon firm adherence to God's word and deference to the church's magisterium, whose duty it is to interpret authentically the word of God.

Defending this exercise of central control, and reaffirming the necessity of the doctrine of infallibility that accompanies it, the current pope insists nonetheless that these actions are not antiecumenical:

> If authority is obliged to intervene, it is not acting against the ecumenical movement but is bringing to this movement its contribution by warning that certain shortcuts do not lead to the goal sought.

However, the numerous warnings and censurings of Catholic scholars, of which the cases of Hans Küng and the corporate admonishing of the Jesuits are only the most visible, have in fact had a chilling effect on ecumenical dialogue. The American Catholic press has been chastised collectively just for publishing open disagreement on church issues, thus, charges Rome, showing "lack of respect for the teachings and decisions of the magisterium." Although John Paul characterizes himself as midway between the extremes of progressivism and traditionalism (or integralism), the impression is abroad in the ecumenical movement that he inclines noticeably to the latter side. One might characterize the current Vatican position as an irenic spirit contained, perhaps paradoxically, in a rather narrow and traditional definition of the way and the goal.[10]*

The World Council, for its part, has accepted only reluctantly the death of the Catholic membership question, and its spokesmen are likely to seek occasions to remind the ecumenical fellowship of its current imperfections. At the Nairobi Assembly in 1975 the sentence "This Assembly looks forward eagerly to the day when it will be possible for the Roman Catholic Church to become a member of the WCC" was added to the report on ecumenical relations by amendment and vote over the tactical objections of the report committee, which noted the obvious fact that the Catholic Church would not join. And the redoubtable M. M. Thomas, then moderator of the Central Committee, said in his report:

> We look forward not merely to the day when the Roman Catholic Church may become a member of the WCC but to the day when the undivided Church can enable a "pre-conciliar WCC" to disappear.

*The publicity attendant upon John Paul's visit to England, and especially the public observances with the Archbishop of Canterbury, Robert Runcie, with their promise to seek "restoration of full communion," gave a superficial impression of renewed ecumenical impetus. But again we have here a verbal commitment without much real content. What Runcie and John Paul did was to reestablish the Anglican-Roman Catholic International Commission, which had already issued its report, only to have the report substantially rejected by the Vatican Congregation for the Doctrine of the Faith.

A certain openness to the shape of that undivided Church characterizes ecumenical exploration for most participants, for example, the idea of a "conciliar fellowship" where mutual recognition of ministry and sacraments would exist within a framework of separately governed churches. Nairobi pressed the vision of unity without detailing the form of the result. But when the Vatican Secretariat for Christian Unity gave *its* report to the Assembly, it said that "theological and pastoral reasons will require the establishment of certain limits to the common witness we are able to give." And the Fourth Official Report of the Joint Working Group, presented to the Assembly, noted as one of the principal barriers that the Roman Catholic Church sees itself as a "universal fellowship with a universal mission," which would only confuse its faithful by entering a fellowship of churches, plural. Although John Paul has now announced his own visit to the WCC, it was to have taken place (before the postponement caused by the attempt on his life) as an addendum to a trip whose principal purpose was to visit the bishops of Switzerland. One may doubt the substantive value of the occasion, which at the present writing has still to happen.[11]*

One must not oversimplify; for there are Catholics, even in the Vatican but especially outside of it, who are impatient with the slow pace of current ecumenism, just as there are World Council staff people quite content to deal with the Roman Catholic Church at the present arm's-length dis-

---

*The papal visit to Geneva was rescheduled and condensed to twelve hours on 15 June 1982, principally to permit John Paul to address the International Labor Organization. During the visit he found time also for speeches at the headquarters of the International Red Cross and the European Center for Nuclear Research, and for a public mass at a new exposition center, but not for a call at the WCC, though his motorcade passed within yards of the Ecumenical Center several times during the day. Nor, so far as I know, did he meet with any officers of the WCC, though I am told that General Secretary Potter and some others attended the public mass. A papal visit to the WCC *may* happen in 1983. But for the present this ordering of priorities, this choice of symbolism, whoever is responsible for it, is clearly a poor portent for ecumenism.

tance. But wherever the cautions and hesitations lie, they are strong enough to have slowed the ecumenical advance. And when one looks for the places where this decline of ecumenism is most marked, it appears, surprisingly, that social questions have become one of the principal stumbling blocks.

Once upon a time, in the infancy of the ecumenical movement, the action wing known as Life and Work had taken as its slogan "Doctrine divides, but service unites." It seemed reasonable in 1925 to look for greater Christian unity in action than in theology. But now, ironically, ecumenical work on doctrine seems more promising and even comfortable than the prickly and embarrassing social questions. For despite the emerging papal conservatism, theologians who wrestle with the doctrinal questions have accomplished some remarkable breakthroughs—sufficient that one may hope that recent warnings and hesitations will in the end prove to have been only temporary setbacks. But the matter is otherwise with social questions. One might have thought, as the bishops' synod did in 1971, that cooperation for development, peace, and human rights would be straightforward enough.[12] It turned out, however, as John Paul acknowledged, that "deep division . . . still exists over moral and ethical matters," which is crippling to Christian unity.[13] We might even reverse the old slogan to describe the current relations of the Roman Catholic Church to the WCC: Common study on doctrine has turned out to be surprisingly fruitful, but common witness on social questions has proved extremely divisive.

Evidently if we could understand the sources of the difficulty, we might improve the situation and so make a considerable contribution to ecumenical relations. But it is not a simple matter to dig out the reasons. Certainly there have been Catholics, notably in Sodepax and Justice and Peace, who desired more of a common witness with the World Council than it has been possible to achieve. The sources of estrangement do not lie in these personalities, but in complex matters of theological method and structure, which in turn feed some differences on the substance of certain issues. The pages that follow explore these sources.

Chapter 1

METHODOLOGICAL DIFFERENCES

Ways of Doing Ethics

The methodological difference most often mentioned is the Roman Catholic preference for relating positions on social questions to the tradition of natural-law ethics, and the World Council's predilection for discovering the divine revelation in the freshness and uniqueness of each event. Of course, these standard, rounded generalizations have their faults. The place of natural law is challenged within Catholic circles, and the World Council's large Orthodox component does not come bearing the so-called Protestant tradition of an ethic of the contextual divine word. Nevertheless, stereotypes do not usually come into being without referring to some large truth, and such is the case here.

The World Council has been called more an organism than an organization, something that has grown in response to stimuli, exercising a ministry of need. It is a ministry which, to quote the constitution of its Churches' Commis-

9

sion on International Affairs (CCIA), "necessitates engagement in immediate and concrete issues as well as the formulation of general Christian aims and purposes." The emphasis is on specific ways of Christian action in specific situations.[14] The Uppsala committee on the CCIA actually expected methodological agreement with the Roman Catholic Church:

> In terms of approach there seem to be strong similarities between their thinking and ours. The approach should be, not so much by formal structures and protocol, as by step-by-step experimentation, and by dealing *ad hoc* with common opportunities as they arise.[15]

But this proved an incorrect assessment of Catholic method.

Statements on social matters from the World Council's Central Committee do indeed seem to rise from a particular incident—say, for example, the Middle East crisis—to a general principle, for example, national territorial integrity, where the enunciation of the principle is clearly influenced by the circumstances that gave rise to it. This gives the unfortunate impression that the World Council is primarily a social action organization that slights the theological component in Christian ethics. This impression is heightened by the news media, which give attention to political statements and activities while slighting the less newsworthy theological work. It is not surprising that critics, including Catholic critics, think of World Council statements as belonging more to the political order than to the moral order—political and economic judgments clothed in the mantle of religious ethics. Because of its penchant for particularity, it makes many more statements than the Vatican, adding to the impression that politics take precedence over theology. The statements it makes, critics acknowledge, may be quite true, justified as political judgments, and yet not be what the Church as *Church* should be doing. It is morally good to be engaged in secular pursuits—St. Thomas would have said as much—but this style blurs the distinction in the Roman Catholic mind between secular judgments and sacred judgments.

The World Council is not insensitive to such criticism, but in its own understanding it means to integrate study and action. This is the action-reflection model of Christian ethics in which action stimulates and guides study as well as vice versa.[16] Certainly the method is not above reproach and has its critics within the World Council as well as without. Even M. M. Thomas, in 1969 when he was chairman of the Central Committee, noted a need for "clearer enunciation of criteria for taking positions and action by the WCC" in international affairs.[17] Yet it is a viable model with a history in Christian ethics, defended as the characteristic biblical method, where theology emerges not systematically but as reflection on concrete situations.[18] The result is not random action, either. It is probably fair to say that there is a touchstone that provides consistency to the World Council's particular and contextual actions, namely, commitment to the poor and oppressed—and no one would deny that *that* test of action is solidly rooted in the New Testament.

For the Roman Catholic tradition the level of abstraction is higher. Statements deal more with general principles, less with the unique features of particular situations. There are, accordingly, fewer statements. They may be called forth by specific situations and sound particular enough—see *Populorum Progressio,* for example. But they start logically, systematically, from principles developed in the long tradition of Catholic social thought. No matter how particular the occasion of a statement, it will be read and judged as applicable to all similar contexts, past, present, and future—e.g., a statement on revolution in Latin America will be heard as applying to eastern Europe. The shorter World Council tradition is freer of the necessity to relate what it does to the teaching of the past and is not bound by its method to be read in the same way in all contexts.

The Catholic tradition, of course, is that of natural law— Thomistic, structural, and rational. The scriptural injunctions that inspire Christian ethics are carefully integrated with the long tradition rather than "heard afresh in the contemporary context." In theory the Church states the principles, and their application is left to others. If the Church attended too zealously to the application, it would be accused of clericalizing politics—a good argument for making more abstract statements. At any rate a fairly clear contrast with the World Council appears, one that could explain many a difference on issues. For example, there was a failure to agree on a joint statement on the Vietnam War because the World Council wanted to mention the American bombing and the Vatican found that issue too specific.

Yet like all contrasts this one can be overdone. In actual practice the Holy See does not always ignore the task of particular application, which it may accomplish, for example, by directing a nuncio to pass on a quiet word. It knows how to prescribe in great detail when it wishes to, for example, the rules for Catholic hospitals. And it generally wants the *right* to intervene specifically, even if it does not do so. In the theory, too, there is room for specificity; for the natural law that lies at the base of Catholic moral teaching is always to be "illuminated and enriched by divine Revelation," which means in practice that "the teaching authority of the Church is competent to interpret even the natural moral law."[19] Also orthodox Thomism is less dominant now, and there is uncertainty within Catholic thought about the foundations of social ethics. Catholic priests in other parts of the world have developed their own style of action-reflection ethics.

Within the World Council, on the other hand, for all the critics who see in traditional Catholic methodology the risk of irrelevance and the danger of platitudinous statements, there are other elements who never were hostile to the natural-law tradition and who appreciate the intent of Catholic procedure. From a practical point of view, also, there are those who value the symbolic role of the Holy See and its usefulness in blessing the *general* direction of programs, a blessing to which one may make effective appeal in particular settings. Some take seriously the criticism that political and theological categories are blurred when worldly causes are too quickly legitimized by use of the Bible.[20] Even the action-reflection model has been relatively recently articulated; the World Council's method in the past was a largely unspecified process in which the seeking of consensus before action played a large role. The current popularity of the action-reflection method may be partly a way of escaping the western parliamentary model of voting on resolutions. Instead, it starts with the action of people without trying first to list agreements and refine distinctions. In short, the World Council's methodology is mixed and of uncertain etiology, not wedded exclusively to a single style that sets it forever apart from the Roman Catholic Church, although current differences in practice are readily discernible.

The Effect of Ideology

There is a further divisive methodological or procedural issue in the role of ideology in formulating Christian social judgments. The apostolic letter *Octogesima Adveniens* of 1971 sharply criticizes "Marxist ideology," "liberal ideology," and "revolutionary ideologies" in general, in part, of course, for reasons of their particular content but also notably because the social teachings of the church should be flexible and not "authenticate a given structure or. . . propose a ready-made model" or "put forward a solution which has universal validity."[21] There is a fair amount of irony here, since many would say that the articulated

Catholic natural-law tradition is itself a "given structure" claiming "universal validity." The World Council, on the other hand, should be protected by its flexible contextualism from according universal validity to any ideology, and thus meet the intent of *Octogesima Adveniens*.

Yet of course the issue between the Holy See and the World Council here is precisely that the latter has listened to revolutionary ideology, and sympathized much with those Christians, including Catholics, who have found in Marxism a powerful tool on the side of the poor and oppressed. For them it is a commitment whose ethical passion is its Christian justification, quite apart from its economic and political analysis. The Church ought not necessarily to take ideological sides, but it must recognize the positive uses of ideology for justice and acknowledge the ideological component already present in Christian thinking. A non-Christian ideology cannot be accepted as a secular faith, but may often be welcomed as a weapon for social change.[22]

If the role of ideology is ambivalent for the World Council, it is positively threatening to the Holy See. Fearing the impact of Marxism in Italy and the defection of militant priests in Latin America, the Vatican views such an ideological commitment as a challenge to the transcendence and ultimacy of Christian teaching, and hence incompatible with it. Catholic documents, particularly the speeches of Pope John Paul II as he travels to various Third World countries, reflect this fear. A commitment to the liberation of the poor and the defense of their rights is put reasonably strongly, but drawn solely from the gospel to the exclusion of any contribution from "ideological systems," i.e., Marxism.[23] The specific content of Marxist ideology is attacked, sometimes directly, more often in oblique references to "certain ideologies." It is condemned for "its atheistic materialism, its dialectic of violence, the way it absorbs individual freedom in the collectivity, at the same time denying all transcendence to man . . . ," for its doctrine of class war, and of course for its oppression of religion. It is wrong to think we can accept Marxism on one level and reject it on others, for all are bound together and end in a "totalitarian and violent society."[24]

Salvation and Liberation

In this insistence on a strict separation between Christian faith and any aspect of a historical ideology, we meet that dimension of Catholic thought often called, whether in praise or blame, "otherworldly," and contrasted with the "this-worldly" activism of the World Council. This distinction is such an old cliché that one advances it with some hesitation, and yet there is something to it after all. Roman Catholicism has been traditionally reluctant to identify salvation with any intramundane liberation. Salvation is not historically immanent, does not deal with the material situation, but is beyond all temporal hopes. The kingdom of God is reached by faith and membership in the Church, not "by the mere changing of structures and social and political involvement." It should not be interpreted "as being present wherever there is a certain type of involvement and activity for justice." The Church's commitment to the needs of the disinherited notwithstanding, "it is wrong to state that political, economic, and social liberation coincides with salvation in Jesus Christ." "This idea of Christ as a political figure does not tally with the Church's catechesis." "[Christ's] mission was not in the social, economic, or political order. Likewise Christ did not give the Church a mission which is social, economic, or political, but rather a religious one."[25]

This conception of the Church as separated from the temporal order is reflected in John Paul's repeated insistence that priests and nuns be a caste apart—"signs and instruments of the invisible world," living among human beings but not *of* this world. Their vocation is unique, possessed of

a singular charism, and should not be touched by seculariz-
ing currents. In particular, its uniqueness should be made
visible to the world by a distinctive religious garb, "an evident sign of complete consecration to the ideals of the
kingdom of heaven, . . . a sign of definitive detachment
from merely human and earthly interests." The Church
apart, served by the caste apart, aspires to no temporal
power or privilege, nor does it oppose civil authority. (It
may thus justly claim freedom from the state's restrictions,
a useful consequence of this otherworldly conception of the
Church and a point obviously on Rome's mind.) John Paul
claims that the direction he has charted is not a reversal of
or recoil from the so-called openness of the Church to the
world set in motion by the Second Vatican Council, especially the council's talk of the common priesthood of the
laity. But to many observers it appears to be just such a
turning back to otherworldliness, a conception in which
many of this pope's themes—insistence on discipline and
loyalty to the pontiff, movement to restrain dissent, emphasis on clerical celibacy as permanent (like the permanence of
marriage, he says), restrictions on the laicization of those
who wish to leave the priesthood, prohibition of non-
Catholic Christians from the Eucharist, and limits on the
forms for mixed marriages—all combine with the general
themes of separation of the Church from the world to form
a consistent picture.[26]

Given its insistence on the sharp distinction between
Church and world, the Holy See would be bound to be sus-
picious of "liberation theology," quite apart from its Marxist component. There are even echoes here of the old dispute
over the relation of the kingdom of God to history, over the
extent to which the transcendence of the kingdom rel-
ativizes historical accomplishments and perhaps drains
them of their urgency. The Vatican may fear that the World
Council is making the old error of liberal theology, which is
to think of worldly betterment as a prelude to the coming
kingdom.

Again, the contrast should not be overdrawn. There are many Catholics now who think in terms of the humanization of this world more than of the perfect other realm that is the soul's destiny. The bishops' synods have been quite direct about declaring that Christian love implies an "absolute demand for justice," and that we must therefore "dedicate ourselves to the liberation of man even in his present existence in this world." Paul VI, who spoke clearly enough of salvation as "transcendent and eschatological," that is, as distinct from material and other temporal needs, nevertheless insisted that this salvation be related to both personal and social life, and include a concern for peace, justice, development, and liberation. Even the current pope, guardedly and with studied ambiguity, will occasionally allow the theological legitimacy of the term "liberation" to include a concern for justice; and he can say that even though "earthly progress must be carefully distinguished from the growth of Christ's kingdom," human advance in this world "even now is able to give some kind of foreshadowing of the new age," and thus "is of vital concern to the Kingdom of God."[27]

Nor is liberal theology regnant within the World Council, where participation in movements for social change is seen as a direct response to the love of Christ, not a precursor of utopia. The World Council may and does make a point of condemning otherworldliness and proclaiming its Christian obligation to be involved in struggles for political and economic liberation, an involvement that manifests the presence of the kingdom among us. But it is as ready as the Holy See to criticize structures and systems as false gods, and equally willing to remind the faithful (though not so often!) that liberation from sin and evil has also a private and eternal dimension. Moreover, the Orthodox tradition, also of course very much a part of the World Council, speaks of the spiritual transformation of humanity rather than of the direct confrontation of structures as the route to salvation—a viewpoint different from either Catholic or most Protestant traditions, and further complicating any effort to describe a neat contrast between the World Council and the Holy See.[28]

Pastoral and Prophetic Styles

Another old typology that is often applied is that of the "priest"—the Catholic approach—against the "prophet"—the World Council's *modus operandi*. The priest has a pastoral function and is responsible for all his people. The Vatican accordingly avoids visible acts whose impact is uncertain and prefers the classic methods of quiet diplomacy. The idea, says John Paul II, is not to "brand and condemn individuals and peoples, but to help change people's behavior and attitudes." So there may be a private letter from the pope to the archbishop of a troubled country, or a private representation of the papal nuncio to the government. The nuncio may be successful in securing the release of political prisoners by such representation, where a public condemnation from the Vatican might serve only to stiffen the defiant resolve of the denounced government. Later, if need be, the Holy See may speak publicly.[29]

This approach involves the Vatican in dealing with the world's powers on particular issues, in spite of its *public* declaration that on social matters it speaks only on general principles. Such a method, priestly and diplomatic, is inherently conservative, disturbing the status quo as little as possible to accomplish its immediate ends. The aim is to humanize the given order.

The prophetic style of the World Council, on the other hand, tends to be less attached to established orders. It is not a church with essentially pastoral functions, but a movement of change, willing to make mistakes as the necessary cost of keeping its dynamism. It *exists* to engage in demonstrative acts, to seize opportunities, to make public pronouncements on specific topics, lest by silence it appear to show unconcern. Its condemnations and denunciations are characteristically given to the press. Its tone, like that of its biblical prophetic models, is forceful and often blunt, eschewing the nuanced voice that the Holy See prizes. Its style alone would be an irritant to Rome, even where there was no substantial disagreement on the issue at hand.

Mutual criticism is inevitable. To the Vatican the World Council's frequent rush to the press looks irresponsible, unreflective, and ineffectual. It is like an unsecured cannonball crashing about the deck of the good ship *Oikoumene*. In its emphasis on the prophet's function it forgets that the Church has a pastoral responsibility to care for *all* of its people. When World Council members, like the Moscow patriarchate or German Lutherans, criticize its actions as too specifically political, the protest is understood in Rome. The Vatican also fears the infectious effect the World Council's actions may have on Catholic radicals, so much so that at one point General Secretary Eugene Blake felt the need to reassure Pope Paul, lest the Holy See recoil from the WCC, that the tension between radicals and conservatives was common to almost all churches and was not only a Roman Catholic problem.[30]

The Vatican, by contrast, has in its own eyes the virtue of ministry to *all* peoples, with their varied and even conflicting needs. Its caution is the reflex of accountability. One of the many merits of its style is that it recognizes the limits of church power. It does what can be done, without squandering the Vatican's credibility in hopeless crusades. The papal office still has symbolic power, but that could erode if it were committed too often to lost causes. Better to encourage lay people, their consciences enlightened by the Church's teaching, to act in specific areas of their competence. The Vatican is even reluctant to see local churches or dioceses act politically, even though, or more likely because, their image is often interventionist. John Paul's speeches regularly argue against direct political participation by the clergy; notice, for example, his removal of Father Robert Drinan from the United States Congress, a move consistent with his general policy of sharpening the demarcation between Church and world. The social and political arena should be left to the laity. Priests and nuns should stick to a purely spiritual role and have "no intention of political interference, nor of participation in the working out of temporal affairs." Justice can only be a secondary concern for priests, whose "main service is that of aiding souls to discover the Father. . . ."[31]

The Vatican's critics suspect that secret diplomacy is not nearly as effective as its apologists claim. The Church does not usually have that kind of power any more. Attempts to exercise it involve the Church with the interest of existing power structures and severely compromise its Christian witness. Worse yet there are darker suspicions that in some countries where the churches have been in conflict with the government on issues of social justice the Vatican's secret diplomacy has in fact abandoned the protesting Christians for the sake of its longer term position in that country. "Recognition" becomes more important than speaking out on human rights. The institution's interests take priority over the care of individuals, who may then have only the choice of submission to evil or martyrdom.

Whether or not this last serious charge has any truth in it, the secretive Vatican style can hardly be popular in the World Council. And when that restraint is imposed on organizations like Justice and Peace and Sodepax, their effective cooperation with the World Council fades away, whatever those who serve them might wish. They are reduced to listening, studying, and making proposals, but not to action with their own programs, lest they affect the prophet's mantle and discomfit their priestly superiors. That reinforces the conviction in Geneva that little prophetic Christian action is likely to come from Rome.

Once again some caveats are in order. The Holy See can

speak out when it wants to: Examples that come readily to mind include Uganda under Idi Amin, the rights of Palestinians, religious liberty in Albania, the Argentina-Chile border dispute, condemnation of Franco's execution of terrorists, direct public intervention in Italian politics over divorce and abortion referenda, and criticism of the Israeli bombing of Iraq's nuclear reactor. The record is dotted not only with these specific references but also with some oddly indirect ones that become direct and clear because of the context of the reference, e.g., "that great nation . . . whose extraordinary human richness is famous" for Russia, in a speech defending the right to dissent; or an attack on violence as plain murder in a speech delivered in Ireland; or a reference to human rights in a speech in the Philippines with President Ferdinand E. Marcos present; or references to violations of international law that seemed to the press at least to refer to Iran's seizure of American hostages (John Paul also privately asked Ayatollah Ruhollah Khomeini directly, but in vain, to free them); or another similar reference that seemed to criticize the Soviet Union's invasion of Afghanistan.[32]

For its part the World Council knows the merits of keeping quiet when the occasion warrants. The surprisingly effective mediation in the Sudanese civil war is a case in point; and inevitably there is a lot of silent work that never comes to public documentation, a necessary public modesty. Pastoral, priestly considerations can overrule prophetic ones, and working through regional or national councils of churches may often be more effective than speaking directly in the WCC's own name—and also more comfortable for the member churches, some of which are occasionally uneasy about the World Council's selection of issues and the number of its statements.

Yet despite these caveats the general differences of method between the two are real, the World Council preferring the direct, plain statement, the Holy See the indirect one, crafted with enough oblique wording to allow some face-saving. The reaction to the assassination of Archbishop Oscar Romero of El Salvador is a textbook case of the differences. The pope's telegram of pain called on the people of the country to eschew violence and vengeance, but made no reference to the political context that caused the murder, even though Romero himself had asked President Carter not to send further arms to the Salvadoran government forces. The World Council, on the other hand, in its condemnation of the assassination, made explicit reference to the political struggle, and quoted approvingly a statement from the United States National Council of Churches critical of American arms shipments to El Salvador. Subsequently John Paul condemned the violence of both guerrillas and armed forces, and called for a halt to the influx of arms. But in these, and in similar remarks about Guatemala, he still remains evenhanded and highly generalized, considerably less specific than the World Council, which continues to denounce American aid to the regime. The pope is even less specific than the United States Catholic Conference, which also openly opposes the Reagan administration on arms shipments.[33]

The Polish martial law crisis has put a considerable strain on the traditional Vatican style. One can almost watch John Paul struggling to keep his public remarks on the usual level of abstraction, but gradually yielding to greater and greater specificity, first departing from his prepared texts to voice his exasperation with the Polish and Russian governments in an informal way, then finally coming to direct, explicit, formal criticism of the restraints imposed on the labor union Solidarity and on the Polish people in general—and all the while visibly consulting with the church in Poland as it seeks to deal with the new situation.[34] Whether this development signals a change in Vatican style remains to be seen. But one may guess that it does not, that we have in this instance a pope sorely tried by national loyalties and operating in an atypical manner on this one issue, undoubtedly in the process making the curial staff nervous. In the long run there is more at issue here than the personality of a particular pontiff, and a methodological convergence with the WCC is still unlikely. The different ways of dealing with the world's troubles are built into the two organizations, are characteristic of their nature, and are likely to remain, as they are now, a source of considerable tension and even anger between them.

Chapter 2

STRUCTURAL BARRIERS

Church and Council

It is not only their methods that separate the Holy See and the World Council in social matters but also their structure. In the first place one is a church, the other a council of churches. The organizations are not parallel. They are designed to do different things, to behave differently. The Vatican is the central office of a single church, and a church, moreover, with an ecclesiology that stresses its unity and centralization despite the many regional variations in Catholicism. It is organic and heirarchical. It speaks authoritatively to its members, who are in theory bound to obey. As a practical matter it cannot prescribe everything, and is probably wiser to leave local churches and the faithful a fair amount of latitude. But nevertheless it exercises an authoritative office, and so its freedom is rather restricted. It has to be cautious and can ill afford to risk errors that might harm its long-term effectiveness. Institutional protectiveness colors its actions, a concern that is not unappreciated in the World Council despite the latter's very different priorities and possibilities.

The statements of the Holy See, not surprisingly, are likely to come, if they come at all, only at the end of a long and arduous process, and to tend toward generalities. The Vatican must keep in mind the effect of its actions on the local churches, which cannot disavow its directives. Often it is safer to say nothing or to speak vaguely. Here again one notices the constraints imposed by the Vatican's pastoral responsibilities. Its close relation to its churches shows in another way when local bishops insist, as they often do, that the Vatican take the lead on difficult issues. In effect, the local people "pass the buck" to Rome in order to avoid having to make the decision themselves. But then that decision from Rome, when it comes, must be aware of local sensibilities.

This cautious manner of dealing with issues may have an effect on relations with the World Council. At least some people have detected a Catholic reluctance to agree to an ecumenical document lest they be committed to it. Keeping the World Council at arm's length, or a conference table's length, becomes a way of life. Fear of being obligated can, however, be simply an excuse for avoiding closer involvement with the World Council, whose own members are not, after all, obligated by its positions.

There, of course, is the principal consequence of the structural difference. The World Council does not speak *for* its members and acts for them only in matters they entrust to it. They are not obligated to accept its judgments.[35] They can and frequently do disassociate themselves from its statements, which are issued in its own name. A loose confederation, it speaks formally at the highest level through the assembly or central committee; but the authority of the pronouncements

will consist only in the weight which they carry by their own truth and wisdom, and the publishing of such statements shall not be held to imply that the World

Council as such has, or can have, any constitutional authority over the constituent churches or right to speak for them.[36]

Lower bodies within the World Council may also speak, but only in their own name. Member churches are left free. The World Council does not direct them or even offer them guidelines, quite unlike the relation of the Holy See to local Catholic churches. Most of the World Council's *program* work—the project help that accounts for most of its budget—is offered to the churches as "enabling" assistance, worked out with their cooperation and carried out through them according to their needs and wishes. It simply does not order or even instruct from above.[37]

This situation gives the World Council a certain free space in which to operate when it does undertake action on its own. Because it does not speak for its member churches, and because they are not held responsible for its actions, it can afford experimental actions, even radical trials. And yet, ironically, there are places where the World Council is more limited than the Holy See. On family issues, for example, the constituency of the World Council is itself so divided that declarations from the central organizations tend to be fairly guarded, whereas for the Vatican these particular issues are matters of Catholic doctrine and accordingly spelled out in detail, legislated for all time. The "resolutions machinery" of the WCC's Central Committee is, in general, on all issues constrained much more by the politics of consensus than is the "magisterial machinery" of the Holy See, which can and does teach against the wishes of sizeable parts of its own constituency.

The World Council can be limited in other ways, too. Its Churches' Commission on International Affairs, for example, must work with the national council of churches in a country where it is dealing with that national government and may act against that council's desires "only on issues of

extreme urgency"—for which action, of course, the national council will not be responsible.[38] On the other side of
the fence, the statements of the Holy See may carry less
authority now than they did before Vatican II, and it may be
that they bear less of a magisterial burden than formerly. So
the image of a freely experimental WCC and a cautiously
responsible Vatican may be subject to modification.

But for the moment it is obvious that these different
kinds of organization will, by their very nature, have difficulty cooperating, if that means operating in parallel ways.
Catholics who function at some distance from the Holy See,
like the Catholic members of the World Council's Faith and
Order Commission, have less difficulty working ecumeni-
cally because bilateralism is not involved. They do not commit the authority of the Roman Catholic Church, do not
make it bear coresponsibility for the results. Nor do they
raise that shadowy but persistently difficult question of why
a Church which claims that the fullness of the faith subsists
in it, which emphasizes its own self-sufficient identity and
initiative, can have anything to learn or gain by working as a
Church in parity with other churches. Unfortunately, on the
other hand, Catholics whose voice invokes the authority of
the magisterium are constrained in precisely these ways. A
statement from Justice and Peace comes from the Vatican,
with weight; it cannot be the same kind of thing as a statement from the CCIA. Two ways of speaking are involved,
which one might call authoritative and provocative.
Perhaps both are necessary, but they are seldom identical.

The Church as State

Another organizational matter of some consequence is
the fact that the Vatican is technically a state as well as the
common name for the central office of a Church. The legal-
ities are subtle and bound up with the particular history of
the conflict between the Papal States and the emergence of

the modern nation of Italy. To be precise, one must say that the 1929 treaty that created the sovereign state of Vatican City was concluded between Italy and the Holy See, the latter thus functioning as a legal personality prior to the emergence of its own territorial state. Technically one should say not that the Holy See *is* a state, but that it *has* or *makes use of* a state called Vatican City. Nevertheless in common practice the Holy See and the Vatican state are indistinguishable. In consequence, it has some of the formal apparatus of a nation, notably, a diplomatic corps with accreditation to many other governments. It can enter into treaties—concordats—with other nations. It enjoys special status at the United Nations and may be a member of some of the specialized U.N. agencies.[39]

How much good this status does may be disputed. The perils of status seeking and secret diplomacy have already been noted. A church that appears and acts on the international stage as another sovereign state too easily becomes embroiled in the politics of nations, exaggerates its institutional interests, and loses its character as a church, particularly one which aspires, as Pope John Paul II regularly reminds us, to identify with the poor and oppressed. On the other hand, if this special juridical status of the Holy See really *can* be made to serve justice and peace, perhaps it is worth preserving. It is said that Roman Catholic diplomats have done much good in Chile and Brazil, and that the nuncios helped prepare the changed relationship of the Spanish episcopate to the new democratic state, well in advance of the reluctant Franco-era bishops. Examples like these show that the Vatican diplomatic system can be useful, though that depends on the specific people operating it. Better to change them, it has been argued, than to abandon the system. Recent popes have defended it along such utilitarian lines, arguing variously (and somewhat self-consciously) that Vatican sovereignty assures freedom for the Holy See's *spiritual* mission, assures its disinterestedness in international politics, and preserves its freedom of action.[40]

The World Council, since it is not a state, is related to nations and to the United Nations as a nongovernmental organization. It cannot pretend to the forms of secular power; but that fact may be counted as virtue. The WCC was free to speak out on the liberation of the Portuguese colonies, while the Vatican was constrained by its concordat with Portugal. The Vatican's diplomatic tie with Taiwan is, apparently, one of the causes of the continuing separation of the mainland Chinese "Patriotic" Catholic Church from Rome, an example of the kind of structural liability unknown to the World Council. Without institutional interests to protect, the World Council gains in credibility. The Sudanese mediation mentioned above, and the Iraq government's permission to the CCIA to inspect Kurdish areas after the civil war, where even the Red Cross was not allowed, show the possibilities open to an organization that lacks the conventional forms of power.

This further difference between the Vatican and the World Council may have a negative impact on their relation when they address an issue jointly. Many people in the World Council appear to believe that the Vatican is reluctant to collaborate for fear of compromising the behind-the-scenes work of its diplomatic personnel or endangering its status in international conferences. The Bucharest population conference of 1974 was preceded by cooperative exchanges between the two bodies, but at the conference itself the Vatican delegates turned their backs on the World Council representatives. The composition of the Vatican delegation, I am told, was a matter of contention in Rome. The people chosen were given strict orders, and were actually afraid of collaboration with the WCC. But beyond their substantive differences over the theme of the conference, part of the problem lies in the different formal relations of the parent bodies to the United Nations, so that their delegates have a different status at conferences.[41] Partaking of this special standing, established in a time when the Roman Catholic Church made exclusive claims, the Holy See finds itself formally isolated from other churches in the international context. Of course this particular point does not apply where it is Catholic *non*governmental organizations that work with the WCC.

The Dynamics of Bureaucracy

Still another source of difficulty resides in the dynamics of bureaucracy. The creation of cooperative structures can actually have a counterproductive effect when they are seen as duplicating work already being addressed in the parent bodies. Instead of facilitating cooperation, they become third forces interposed between the similar organizations in Rome and Geneva. Sodepax was, of course, the classic instance. With a large budget from external sources supporting an independent-minded director, it was from its inception a freewheeling operation, worrisome to its creators, perhaps especially to the Vatican. For the World Council the trouble was not so much the independence of Sodepax's work and judgments, but its potential for overlapping and eroding existing structures.

Not surprisingly, then, Sodepax soon found itself cut back and restricted, mainly from the Vatican side, but with the World Council acquiescing.[42] Its initial dynamism was lost. Its director, George Dunne, a Jesuit, was replaced and its program subjected to closer control by the parent bodies. It was criticized for its direct contact with local churches and for the frequency of publication of its journal *Church Alert*. The Vatican even objected to opinion articles in the journal, preferring to limit it to official statements. In fact, Rome wished to reduce Sodepax even further, making it a mere liaison for exchange of information without any outreach to the churches. This exercise of Roman central control extended also to Justice and Peace, which went through a period of uncertainty about its status after its first director, Monsignor Joseph Gremillion, resigned. It has now been definitively established with a very limited role related more to Catholic institutional concerns like evangelism than to ecumenical cooperation and outreach.[43]

The Christian Medical Commission is another example of a cooperative structure with identity problems. Unlike Sodepax, it is not a joint product of the Vatican and the World Council; but its purpose of recommending ways of joint planning and action for better use of health-care resources led to the early inclusion of Catholic members and eventually of a Catholic staff person. Vatican support, however, has been only lukewarm, at least in the perception of many people who have worked for the CMC. Again the problem is the relative independence of the organization, which is beyond effective control from Rome, and the presence of an at least partially overlapping institution within the Catholic Church, Cor Unum (though Cor Unum has a broader coordinating function).

The World Council has been critical of such bilateral structures because, it is said, they function as a substitute for full membership of the Roman Catholic Church in the WCC. Cooperative bodies enable the Vatican to function as if it were a member, in areas of its concern, and remove any further incentive to join. "Bipolar structures have a paralyzing effect," and institutionalize nonmembership.[44] Also, of course, the World Council loses its initiative and possibility of decision in such restrictive joint bodies, which further accounts for the ambivalence in its own support of them.

The Holy See's objection to these bodies is not their stultifying effect on membership, which the Vatican does not desire anyway, but the possibility that they will generate independent programs. They are acceptable only under control; and when, like Sodepax and the CMC, they are housed in Geneva, it is at least conceivable that they will reflect more of the World Council than of the Roman Catholic

Church. If they cannot be controlled, it is perhaps best for the Vatican if Catholic participation in them is minimal. So the parent bodies reach similar conclusions for different reasons; and it is not surprising that a proposal to transform the CMC into a jointly sponsored body like Sodepax was buried.

An institution under control means one with a restricted function, like the exchange of information. And this indeed seems to be the direction of the Vatican's participation with the World Council in social matters. But even on this level there are problems. The complaint is widespread that the information flow is largely one way, from Geneva to Rome. The CMC complains that Cor Unum does not share its own studies, e.g., on the Church as a healing community or on the handicapped, but seems quite content to take material from the CMC to use as its own and to send representatives to CMC meetings without reciprocating the invitation. Likewise Sodepax feared that its reduction to liaison status would mean that it would exist primarily to collect papers for Justice and Peace; and the latter, as part of its new restraint, has little information it may pass on to World Council agencies and is no longer allowed to invite World Council observers to its annual meeting. From the CCIA, from the Urban Industrial Mission, from Church and Society, the same complaint is heard: no feedback from Rome, simply the receipt of World Council information to be used for the Vatican's own purposes, and sometimes as the basis of its own literature.

Against this rather bleak picture there are reports of extensive and growing cooperation on the field, in many different localities—Action for Food Production (AFPRO) in India, joint Christian Medical Commissions in several countries, human-rights agencies in Latin America, among many examples. The Roman Catholics are even members of the national council of churches in several countries. Often enough the pattern is one where World Council-supported agencies receive full cooperation from local Catholic churches or orders. Sometimes these churches or orders are intentionally bypassing Rome. Sometimes there is tacit Vatican approval, but hardly more than that. There seems to be considerable feeling that it is World Council, or at least Protestant, aid that sustains most of these local cooperative ventures receiving outside support. There are signs here and there of local Catholic cooperation being withdrawn at the behest of higher authority. Predictably the cooperation is uneven, with the minority party in any venture often reluctant and fearful of losing its identity. Real joint programs require real fellowship; a shared sense of unity is the precondition of genuine cooperation, and that has yet to be achieved.

Internal Tensions

Finally, in this list of structural or organizational factors inhibiting ecumenical cooperation, one should note the internal condition of the Roman Catholic Church. The period since Vatican II has been very unsettled, producing a crisis of identity and authority that has complicated ecumenical relations. The changes set in motion by the great council, so widely and deservedly praised, have been ill absorbed in the Church. The status given to national conferences of bishops and the new concept of collegiality have introduced decentralization into a body used to central authority. The new initiatives granted to the laity have limited the scope of clerical authority and reduced the dependence of the faithful on instruction from the top. The impulse the council gave to ecumenism was great, but led some people to go further on their own, even to intercommunion. There have been defections of clergy, the appearance of quasi-heretical writings among some of them, a falling off of religious practice, and noisy controversies over contraception, over celibacy of priests, over the status of women, over liberation theology.

Naturally there have been negative conservative reactions of varying degrees. The Holy See was doubtless surprised and frightened by the intensity of the most extreme reactions, like the Lefèbvre affair, and by the degree of support they received among the laity. There have been tensions with the orders and with local dioceses. Of course, not all of those disconcerted have been more conservative. Some have been more liberal; and the Vatican often finds itself caught between opposing forces—e.g., more liberal than the Portuguese or Polish hierarchy, less liberal than the Americans or Dutch or Brazilians or South Africans. In any event the situation is a crisis of authority and credibility for Rome, and the concomitant tendency to decentralization has added to the problem.

So the Vatican must walk softly and very carefully if it is not to exacerbate these divisive tendencies. A decisive and dramatic move might split the Church. No wonder that it is cautious and noncommital in dealing with the World Council and shies away from a move toward membership that would surely alienate much of its constituency. No wonder that the popes are critical of liberation theology and Marxism, and that the Vatican Secretariat of State reins in Justice and Peace. This is not a time to have organizations on the cutting edge of social change.

Besides the general malaise of the years since Vatican II, certain particular factors have played a role in Rome's wariness. The volatile Italian political situation, with the possibility of a Communist government or of anarchy, has affected the actions of the Vatican in a politically conservative direction. Its diplomatic corps, heavily Italian, possessing the power to interfere in the affairs of local churches, has been a source of reaction in many cases, by reason of its composition more than by the fact of its existence. The character of Pope Paul, too, played a part. Most of my informants, though not all, spoke of him as conservative— a mood already present in 1969 so far as relations with the

World Council were concerned. He was consistently pessimistic in his speeches about the dangers of the new forces besetting the Church. Sensitive and responsive to the theological traditionalism in the curia, he was, because of the infirmities of old age, increasingly reluctant to undertake or sanction new ventures. With the advent of John Paul II the uncertainties of the end of a pontificate have been replaced by the different uncertainties of the beginning of a new one. A new pope is a mystery for a while, and new ecumenical initiatives are likely to await the formation of the new papal style and priorities. As if all these historical accidents were not enough, there may even be another source of ecumenical trouble in the dominance of different types of culture in each organization—a Vatican dominated by Latin peoples trying to deal with a World Council dominated (though increasingly heterogeneous) by northern peoples.

In some measure the general forces causing unrest in the Roman Catholic Church have also affected the World Council. For both this is a time of questioning advances so far undertaken, of dealing with critical conservative forces, and, for the "liberals" of both sides, of trying simply to maintain what has already been accomplished. For structural reasons already discussed, the problem is more acute for the Catholic Church. But awareness of its own inner tensions may help the World Council, without muting the necessary criticism, to a more sympathetic understanding of the Vatican's difficulties.

Chapter 3

SUBSTANTIVE ISSUES

Given the considerable differences between the World Council and the Holy See in matters of method and structure, we need now to inquire whether ecumenical relations are further complicated by *substantive* disagreement on major social questions. Let us begin this inquiry in the general area of human rights.

Human Rights, Religious Liberty

In the Roman Catholic tradition human rights are based on the natural law and are discoverable by universal human reason. The natural law, since it is the reflection of the mind of God in created things, applies equally to all people everywhere, and can be known by all rational beings. Of course, as something coming from the mind of God, it is specifically confirmed in Christian revelation. It is concerned above all with individuals—with their temporal welfare and eternal destiny. The primacy of the individual is secured theologically by the doctrine of human creation in the image of God, by the incarnation of God in human form, and by the redemption wrought in Christ. It is to the individual person, whose soul is dear to God, that unalienable rights belong.

Of course, possessing a universal right entails respecting that right in other people. We are bound to one another in community and must not indulge in selfish individualism. Happily, defense of individual rights also tends to produce a healthy community. In any case there are some rights that ought never to be suspended for the sake of the social good—e.g., the prohibition on killing innocent people—while others may be restrained in their exercise, though not eliminated, for the sake of community—e.g., the right to hold private property. In the inevitable tension between individual and community one must remember that the community exists to protect and fulfill the individual:

> Human personality. . . is an ontological and psychological reality which is autonomous in the civil sphere. Within its own sphere its liberty and basic rights take precedence in certain cases over social and political structures. The teaching of the magisterium stresses the primacy of the person as the goal of social institutions.[45]

Rights so derived apply also to groups, communities, peoples; so that in defending them, the Church speaks not only to the defense of individuals but of "social justice, the development of peoples, . . . war and peace, and racism."[46] The concept of rights is thus given a very broad application, broader perhaps than some would like who would distinguish social goals or aspirations from fundamental human rights. The teaching does cast a wide net, and catches up in its concern "rights of association, marriage, and family, participation in public affairs, work, private property, education, development, . . . the right to emigrate, . . . the right to asylum," the right to life (including fetal life), to a decent standard of living, to literacy, to cultural identity, to voting and participation in decision making, to dissent for reasons of conscience, to equality before the law, to personal dignity, to physical and psychological integrity (including the condemnation of torture), and, of course, to religious liberty. With a list that long, and expandable at that, it is not surprising that current Catholic teaching endorses the U.N. Universal Declaration of Human Rights, defends the Helsinki accords, and calls upon nations to ratify the covenants on economic, social, and cultural rights, and on civil and political rights.[47]

The matter of religious liberty is, understandably, of special concern to the Vatican. Whatever the Church's record in the past, it is now a full supporter of the idea whether Catholicism be dominant or, as is often the case today, struggling under oppressive governments:

> Everyone has the right to worship God according to the right norm of his own conscience, to practice his religion both in private and in public, and to enjoy religious liberty.[48]

More broadly, the definition includes the right of religious education and the right to seek truth:

> No power on earth has the right to prevent people from searching for truth, from receiving it freely, from knowing it fully, and from openly and freely professing it.[49]

And ultimately religious liberty is singularly important as "the basis of all other liberties."[50]

The WCC is heir to a more varied tradition of human rights, according to the diversity of its membership. It has, for example, the Anglo-Saxon tradition stressing an individualism derived from the natural-law tradition, and the continental Reformation tradition emphasizing the primacy of the community of mutual service, where individuals are said to have their existence essentially in relation to others. In its declarations the World Council draws on different strands, and the result in practical terms is not unlike the Catholic teaching. The *Uppsala Report* grounds human rights and full equality in the "inherent dignity of man," echoing language from the Universal Declaration about the "inherent dignity and equal and unalienable rights of all members of the human family." The Central Committee has recently again cited this wording approvingly. In 1971 the Central Committee adopted a memorandum on human rights that included the Universal Declaration as an appendix, and the Executive and Central Committees have urged ratification of the U.N. covenants, noting the right of individuals to appeal internationally from violations of their rights by their own governments. "These principles and standards largely coincide with our current Christian understanding about what makes up a just society."[51]

Like the Holy See, the World Council extends rights to classes and groups, considering poverty and political oppression as violations of basic rights:

> The rights of the individual are inherently bound up with the struggle for a better standard of living for the underprivileged of all nations. Human rights cannot be safeguarded in a world of glaring inequalities and social conflict.[52]

In fact there are some signs of restiveness with the individualistic and thus apolitical basis of the U.N. view of rights, which may not take sufficiently into account the social and political context of individual life.[53]

Again like the Vatican, the World Council ranges far and wide in applying its sense of rights. It denounces as violations a long list of particular abuses, such as arbitrary arrest and detention, capital punishment, stiff punishment for political dissenters, imprisonment of conscientious objectors to particular wars, torture, suppression of cultural identity, denial of participation in decision making, and much more, with a cumulative effect much like that of the Vatican's statements. Here, too, social goals as well as political liberties have the status of human rights: work, food, health care, housing, and education are part of the right to life.[54]

On religious liberty the World Council is substantially at one with the Holy See, supporting the applicable provision in the Universal Declaration and urging a U.N. covenant on the subject. The Central Committee could actually criticize the shortcomings of a particular law in Spain by pointing out its inadequacy not only in terms of the Universal Declaration but also in terms of the statements of Vatican II, whose standards are cited approvingly. Religious liberty, says the World Council, is not a matter of special privilege, but a right of all religious communities:

> . . . the freedom to have or to adopt a religion or belief of one's choice, and freedom, either individually or in community with others and in public or private to manifest one's religion or belief in worship, observance, practice, and teaching,

including the right to criticize the ruling powers on the basis of religious conviction. Religious freedom needs active attention and defense because it is fundamental to other rights and all too often violated even today, e.g., where religious revival "in some parts of the world" causes tension among religious communities. (The reference is mainly to Moslem fundamentalists in many areas. Their militance caused the removal of the fifth assembly of the WCC from Jakarta to Nairobi.)[55]

For differences between the Holy See and the World Council on human rights we must look mainly to the *application* of their convictions. The Vatican, true to its preferred method, denounces the sin and not the sinner, states the principle without pointing by name at the place where it is violated. The World Council in its prophetic style starts with a concrete example, speaks to that issue, and names the principle involved. The Vatican shies away from scolding particular governments, and restrains its local clergy from doing so where it can. Polish bishops have supported workers against the government, and Latin American bishops have championed human rights against *their* governments; but they act on their own authority (though the sympathy of the present Polish pope for the cause of the Polish workers was openly expressed even before martial law banned Solidarity and has been made even more explicit since then). The Vatican seems to prefer local *pastoral* action, mainly educational, even though in theory corporate witness by the Church for human rights, including active protest, is acceptable. Papal speeches may be *interpreted* as specifically critical in the context where they are delivered, as noted above, e.g., the speech before Philippine President Marcos; but the words read literally are abstract defenses of human rights in general.[56]

The World Council's actions by contrast come directly from the central body, speak to a particular problem, and are public. So it declared for a "more just and equitable society" in Northern Ireland; for a full political role for blacks in Zimbabwe/Rhodesia; for the right of Palestinians to self-determination and a place in direct peace negotiations (although it deplored the Munich Olympic killings); for the rights of Indians in Uganda; against Idi Amin's "six-year reign of terror" there, especially the murder of Anglican Archbishop Janani Luwum; for fairness in the Soviet government's treatment of religious dissidents and others whose alleged "crimes" are often only public defense of human rights; and for free elections in Namibia. The WCC has spoken for assistance to refugees in Burma, southern Africa, Vietnam, Nicaragua, and elsewhere; for the right of refugees to leave and to voluntary repatriation, and, while acknowledging the problems for host countries, for resettlement if the refugees cannot return (though recent emphasis is on preventing causes that create refugees in the first place). It has made statements favoring the release of the American hostages in Iran and on behalf of rights for political dissenters in Chile, the Philippines, Korea, Argentina, southern Africa, Iraq, India, Bolivia, Ethiopia, Taiwan, and wherever the crisis of the moment is. And this is only a bare sample of the WCC's activity.[57]

Choosing specific targets in this manner leaves the World Council vulnerable to the charge of "selective indignation": why these particular declarations and not others? In fact, the World Council frankly admits that to protect some victims, or even its member churches, against government reprisals, it sometimes keeps silent, notably in eastern Europe and parts of Latin America. Disagreement within the Executive or Central Committees has also kept the WCC on occasion from speaking out. The silence is not easily accepted, and some of the fiercest criticism of the World Council's selectivity comes from within. There is constant pressure to stop sheltering any government from deserved criticism—a pressure that has resulted in some carefully phrased compromise statements.[58]

The Vatican, of course, is open to the opposite charge of an indignation so general that violators of rights need take no notice nor hardly feel themselves addressed. The situation is the occasion of mutual resentment: The Holy See is critical of the World Council's imbalance, lack of objectivity, and susceptibility to ill-conceived political judgments, while the World Council is angry at the Holy See for evading the difficult particular issues where the Church must risk a government's disfavor in order to defend the victims of injustice. When the World Council is attacked for not speaking out on violations of human rights in eastern Europe because of the political sensitivity of that region, its people are likely to wonder why these critics do not make the same demand of Rome, which avoids particular speaking everywhere. And so ecumenical cooperation is unusual. There are exceptions—the CCIA and Pax Romana joined two secular organizations in presenting a case of alleged torture in Brazil to the U.N. Human Rights Commission in 1971, for example[59]—but these cases are rare. For an area like human rights, where the extent of theoretical agreement between Rome and Geneva is so broad, it is remarkable how much mutual distrust and resentment there is in fact.

Racism

Among human-rights topics racism deserves special mention because it has been such a source of discord between the two organizations. As with the subject of rights generally, the difficulty arises not over theory but practice. The same strong theoretical position is held by both sides. Racial discrimination is "an unutterable offense against God, to be endured no longer" (says the World Council),[60] an "inadmissible affront to the fundamental rights of the human person" (says the Holy See).[61] "All men and women are equal by reason of their common origin, nature, and destiny."[62] The *Uppsala Report* defines racism this way:

By racism we mean ethnocentric pride in one's own racial group and preference for the distinctive characteristics of that group, belief that these characteristics are fundamentally biological in nature and are thus transmitted to succeeding generations; strong negative feelings toward other groups who do not share these characteristics coupled with the threat to discriminate against and exclude the outgroup from full participation in the life of the community.[63]

The Assembly's attitude toward this phenomenon was perfectly clear, and expressed theologically:

Racism is a blatant denial of the Christian faith. It denies the effectiveness of the reconciling work of Jesus Christ, through whose love all human diversities lose their divisive significance; it denies our common humanity in creation and our belief that all men are made in God's image; it falsely asserts that we find our significance in terms of racial identity rather than in Jesus Christ.[64]

Paul VI, quoting *Gaudium et Spes* (a Second Vatican Council document), said:

Since all men possess a rational soul and are created in God's likeness, since they have the same nature and origin, have been redeemed by Christ and enjoy the same divine calling and destiny, the basic equality of all must receive increasingly greater recognition.[65]

Beyond these similar statements the divergences begin with the World Council's habit of applying them critically and prophetically to named particular situations. Such particularism is not entirely absent from Vatican statements: Pope Paul spoke specifically in favor of universal suffrage in southern Africa, for example.[66] But again, such particularity from the Vatican in a public statement is unusual. It is the World Council that names names, listing situations of racial discrimination in southern Africa, the United States, Australia, India, Japan, and New Zealand. It spoke out against the oppression of migrant laborers in western Europe and of tribal and ethnic groups in the new nations of Africa, southeast Asia, and elsewhere. It has been most detailed on southern Africa, calling for an end to the Ian Smith regime in Rhodesia, championing full political participation for the blacks of that country, and speaking openly of the "liberation" of Rhodesia as Zimbabwe. It has supported the recognition of the South-West Africa People's Organization (SWAPO) as "the authentic representative of the people of Namibia" and denounced South African obstruction of the U.N. intentions for the territory (including specifically the military raids into Angola). The WCC has condemned all forms of apartheid and repression of blacks in South Africa (including the creation of black homelands or Bantustans), denouncing western economic links with that country, and even repeatedly opposing the migration of whites away from South Africa as a "transfer of racism to another society" and an attempt to avoid the formation of a just multiracial society, which the World Council regards as the only morally acceptable solution.[67]

The World Council concentrates its attack on the phenomenon of white racism, so widely manifested in the world. But this focus "does not exclude the consideration of various expressions of counter-racism or other forms of racism," which also need to be attacked and broken. And indeed, in its specific condemnations are to be found several examples of nonwhite racism.[68] Nor does the World Council spare the churches themselves, calling for the eradication of the subtle forms of institutional racism that have crept into their own lives. Educational materials, employment and investment policies, and all aspects of church life should be scrutinized for traces of complicity in the perpetuation of racial discrimination—a self-critical dimension that seems lacking in Catholic treatment of the subject.[69]

But it is not just in the particularity of its statements that the World Council's approach to racism differs from the

Vatican's. It is, above all, in the WCC's daring action program that the distinction resides—a distinction that is one of the major points of ecumenical friction. Arguing that only painful sacrificial action would be taken seriously as an attempt to end racism, the World Council in 1969 created its Program to Combat Racism (PCR) as a crash program financed initially with $200,000 from its scarce reserves—a move that made its finance committee very nervous. The commitment was obviously serious, as the money was to be *distributed* to organizations combatting racism, including guerrilla liberation movements "whose purposes are not inconsonant with the general purposes of the World Council." Since its creation the PCR has used a special fund, which receives contributions for this purpose, to continue its support for such liberation movements, including a much publicized and highly controversial grant to the Patriotic Front of Zimbabwe. This aspect of the program has probably earned the World Council more notoriety than anything else it has ever done. The program goes beyond money distribution to include "all the means . . . of political actions towards the bringing about of racial justice, including economic sanctions"—because racism is not only about attitudes but a means to maintain unjust power relations. Toward this end the World Council urged, and continues to urge, the churches to "withdraw investments from institutions that perpetuate racism." The WCC itself took the lead by disposing of its own investments so tainted, e.g., all those involved in business in South Africa—again over the opposition of its finance committee, which preferred stockholder pressure to disinvestment.[70]

Although local Catholic dioceses and orders contributed to the PCR, and the European Conference of Justice and Peace Commissions requested the Pontifical Commission to study the disinvestment resolutions,[71] the program caused great anxiety in the Vatican. Even though the grants to liberation movements were for social, agricultural, educational, and health services, they did, of course, strengthen these movements, some of which were engaged in guerrilla warfare; and the Vatican consistently refuses to sanction violence as a means to social justice. Disinvestment, moreover, would have been a response far too specifically targeted for the Vatican style. My inquiries as to whether data on church investments were actually available for moral scrutiny by Justice and Peace yielded nothing.

The Vatican had the additional complication of its concordat with the Portuguese government, which made exceedingly difficult any relation with the liberation movements in what were then Portuguese colonies. In 1970 three leaders of these movements were received by Pope Paul, who could do no more than stress his *pastoral* responsibility for their supporters. But even that was too much for the Portuguese hierarchy, which was grievously affronted. The PCR, unsympathetic to this indecisiveness on an issue of conscience, accused the Roman Catholic Church of supporting "the oppressive colonialist activities of the Portuguese government," and brought its complaint to the Joint Working Group—"but [to quote the circumspect minutes of the WCC Executive Committee] there was no clear answer as to whether any Roman Catholic body was prepared to take up the matter at the highest level in that church."[72]

All things considered, it is not surprising that on the subject of racism there has been little ecumenical cooperation at the highest levels. It is the experience of the PCR that its proposals for joint study and action—e.g., on racism in textbooks or racism in missionary training—while received sympathetically by Justice and Peace, in fact make no progress and seemed to be blocked at a higher level in the Vatican, probably in the Secretariat of State.

Nationalism

In their defense of human rights both the Holy See and the World Council have been led to champion the proposal for international covenants or other machinery to limit the exercise of national sovereignty. The nation-state must acknowledge that it is subject to higher laws "and should therefore not regard international concern for the implementation of these rights as an unwarranted interference."[73] But it is not just for the cause of human rights that Christian social thought is internationalist. There has always been a sense that national rivalry produces war along with injustice for weaker nations. Hence there has been sentiment in favor of a strong United Nations and other institutions to deal with humanity's problems at the global level. A functioning body of international law and a strengthened United Nations might be able to settle conflicts before they erupted into war, might deal constructively with problems of refugees and migrant labor, and might move effectively against the sufferings caused by natural calamities like drought. In recent years attention has centered also on the problem of economic disparity, which, it is said, can only be corrected by international action:

> The churches should . . . consider how the present economic structures in which national sovereignty plays a decisive role can be transformed into a structure in which decisions affecting the welfare of all are taken at the international level.[74]

Both the Holy See and the World Council are heirs to a tradition of internationalism. Roman Catholic thought has always harbored reservations about the national state, though it has known how to make its peace with individual governments. In part this attitude stems from the accidents of history, the rise of modern nations having often been accompanied by opposition to Rome. But in part Catholic internationalism is also the product of a universal outlook that builds on universal human nature, universal reason, and the universal natural law.

Of course, all Christian thought has a bias toward the universal, confessing that Christ died for all humanity and that God wills love for all human beings. Among the antecedent organizations that joined to form the World Council, the Life and Work movement in particular brought Christian universalism to the study of international relations, and supported with religious fervor the League of Nations and all machinery for adjudicating disputes among nations without force. This spirit, chastened by history but still very much alive, has descended directly to the World Council. The Church must maintain its transcendence over particular cultures and not be identified with any, so that it can speak for world community.[75]

Yet there is also a powerful countercurrent in appreciation of nationalism, and it is noticeably stronger in the World Council than in the Vatican—perhaps in part because the former is only a *council* of churches that are nationally based, not a centralized church spanning frontiers. At any rate the World Council's statements put strong emphasis on the territorial integrity and political independence of nations. It has consistently championed full self-government for colonies. It has denounced foreign interference in internal affairs (Vietnam, Cyprus, and Angola) and the violation of national frontiers (the Soviet invasions of Czechoslovakia and Afghanistan, however carefully the WCC handled them). Up to a point it defends self-determination for ethnic groups that have a strong identity and desire autonomy, e.g., *both* the Palestinians *and* the Israelis. "All people have the right freely to determine their political status and freely to pursue their economic, cultural, and social development," including minorities within nations as well as nations themselves.[76]

There are, however, problems, if not indeed contradictions, in the WCC's support of nationalism. Modern nations usually encompass different ethnic groups. To support autonomy for all of them is to risk destroying the nation, but to deny them self-government is to go against the principle by which nationalism is defended. There are insoluble dilemmas here. The World Council is against "tribal, caste, and other narrow loyalties" that destroy the larger community the nation makes possible; and it is quite opposed to the creation of Bantustans in South Africa. Yet in principle it is for the autonomy of subject peoples. In civil wars like Northern Ireland's or Nigeria's, where one ethnic group charges oppression by another, the World Council is unable to decide between supporting the cause of the secessionists or that of national unity.[77] In international relations it tends to approve national self-assertion exercised by weaker nations, but not that exercised by dominant nations. The *Nairobi Report* tried to distinguish between the kind of nationalism which expresses legitimate cultural integrity and that which distorts and romanticizes indigenous culture.[78] But it is hard to find the thread of principle in all of this, and it may well be that the Holy See is more consistent and more circumspect in treating the self-determination of *all* peoples as a right to be sharply limited by their responsibility for the common good of the whole world.

Yet even the Roman Catholic Church has been touched by the dilemma of a traditional Christian universalism confronted by a resurgent nationalism claiming cultural identity as a necessary condition of human freedom and integrity. Just as with the World Council, it is the new nations of the ex-colonial world that have borne this claim into the councils of the Church. One can sense traditional Catholic reluctance on this point in the 1971 bishops' synod's lukewarm acknowledgement of the legitimacy of "a certain responsible nationalism" to give a people the impetus to develop their own postcolonial identity as a matter of self-determination.[79]

Pope John Paul II seems personally more sympathetic as

a result of his own Polish national pride. In fact, his speeches on his first trip as pope to Poland are striking in their celebration of Poland and of himself as the first Polish pope. He makes a point of the right of nations to cultural and political autonomy, to independence. On the clash of such rights between Israel and the Palestinians over the same territory he is more guarded than the World Council, which has bluntly condemned Israeli annexation of East Jerusalem, thus drawing the wrath of Jewish organizations that defend the right of Jews alone to rule the united city. John Paul is sympathetic to Israel's origins and security needs, but refrains from speaking explicitly of its "rights," is solicitous for the "sad condition of the Palestinian people . . . excluded from their homeland," and continues by implication more than by direct statement the Vatican preference for some form of internationalization of Jerusalem.[80]

It is in the liturgy that the issue of the proper place of cultural particularism within the universal church has been most insistently forced. Of course, in the larger historical perspective the Roman Catholic Church is used to this problem and has adapted itself to local cultures in some ways while maintaining an overarching uniformity. But in places like India and Africa the old question is newly acute. John Paul on his trip to Africa, for example, carefully skirted the challenge of the Zairean rite for the mass, which Rome does not sanction. The Holy See's "solution"—such as it is—is, on the one hand, to say that the universal gospel may take concrete forms that reflect different cultures where it lives, with Rome not dominating or controlling the particular traditions of churches in different nations. On the other hand, the Holy See lifts up and celebrates the elements of local cultures which are said to reflect the natural law, characterizing them as universal despite their particularity. But the critical note remains: the gospel "complements and perfects" culture; it "purifies and transfigures" the local heritage. The accommodation to the ethnic spirit and national cultural celebration is a wary one, warier than that of the World Council.[81]

Violence and Revolution

The subject of war is a perennial controversy in Christian ethics. While pacifism is the most ancient tradition in the Church, it is not the dominant one in either the WCC or the Roman Catholic Church. There are important pacifist elements in both fellowships, and both speak seriously of peace education.[82] But both acknowledge in practice the tradition of a "just war"—a concept that originated in the ancient world outside the Church, but was eventually brought into it and developed there. While the messages from the Holy See tend to echo that tradition in general principles, like the hope for arbitration of quarrels under international law instead of by war,[83] the World Council, as is its wont, reflects the principles without abstracting them, in a flow of statement addressed to particular situations.

Of the historical criteria for a just war, the World Council in the past decade has dealt mainly with two, the need to negotiate in good faith, and the need to observe limited and just methods in fighting. It called repeatedly for negotiations to end the Vietnam War and the Nigerian civil war in keeping with the tradition that resort to arms instead of trying to negotiate invalidates a claim to just cause (*jus ad bellum*). And it has spoken again and again on particular means of conducting warfare, as the tradition requires that weapons and their use must also follow certain limiting rules (*jus in bello*). Accordingly, it denounced the American bombing of North Vietnam, presumably as excessive force whose major impact was on civilian populations. It deplored warfare that deliberately damaged soil and vegetation. It argued for humane treatment of prisoners of war. It urged the Federal Government of Nigeria to stop its blockade of humanitarian relief headed for Biafra. It spoke against chemical-biological weapons and napalm as well as attacks on civilian populations "as such." And, more generally, it adopted its own CCIA's statement on "Limitations in Modern Warfare."[84]

Several attempts have been made to have statements issued jointly by the Vatican and the World Council; all but one were failures. The stumbling block was, as usual, the insistence of the World Council on being specific. As noted earlier, a sustained, serious effort to issue a common declaration on the Vietnam War finally foundered on the World Council's insistence on condemning the American bombing, a judgment much too political and technical for the Vatican generalists. The sole joint statement of the two bodies was a March 1968 call for an immediate end to the war in Nigeria. This was achieved only because General Secretary Blake was so eager to set a precedent of joint declarations that he agreed to avoid specifics in order to secure the Vatican's accord.

Disarmament has been a long-time concern of the churches, and here the Holy See and the World Council are in substantial agreement. Both condemn the arms race unequivocally as not only leading inevitably to the use of the accumulated weapons but also as a diversion of resources from the task of helping the poor. It is a scandal, a piece of madness, a curse. Nuclear weapons in particular as well as other conceivable weapons of mass destruction do not insure security, but rather create the conditions for the destruction of the human race.

Both the Holy See and the World Council acknowledge the need for defensive arms, which is in harmony with the just-war doctrine. But the unchecked proliferation of weapons "for defense," they argue, is actually destabilizing and tends to generate the conflicts it claims to prevent. And if war is unleashed, the damage it will cause if it is fought with the most destructive modern weapons will be dispro-

portionate to any values the arms may have been acquired
to protect. Better to suffer and resort to nonviolent resist-
ance (says the Holy See, at least) than to enter upon such
destruction. Also, a stockpile of arms, even if never fired,
can be used as an instrument of domination by threat and
often enough provokes terrorism in reply. For all these reasons the level of arms must at least be sharply reduced, and
nuclear weapons eliminated altogether, even if ultimately
some minimal defensive requirement will remain.[85]

Pope John Paul II has recently taken what for the Vatican
is the unusually specific step of sending delegations of scientists to the governments of the United States, the Soviet
Union, Great Britain, and France and to the United Nations
with a study by the Pontifical Academy of Sciences to the
effect that nuclear war cannot be "won," and not really
"survived."[86] Of course, even in its specificity this action is
even-handed; and it is left to the World Council, as usual, to
apply to particular instances the general conclusions it
shares with the Holy See. Thus the nuclear nonproliferation
treaty is praised, and nations, especially France and China,
are urged to sign it. (Pope Paul endorsed it "without any
political implications.") The Strategic Arms Limitation
Treaty creates a better atmosphere between the United
States and Soviet Russia and should be ratified. A later decision to deploy NATO nuclear missiles in Europe is deplored, along with the deteriorating relations between the
superpowers that prompted the decision. Existing nuclear
powers should allow nonnuclear nations to share in decisions affecting their own security. Outside nations should
not provide arms to places of conflict lest the war simply be
prolonged, as in the Nigerian civil war or the Middle East.
Nor should they be provided to South Africa lest oppression be strengthened. More recently the development of
new weapons like the American neutron bomb has been denounced as making nuclear war more likely; instead, all nuclear weapons should be eliminated. *Any* tendency toward

thinking *any* kind of nuclear war might be winnable is attacked as dangerous and foolish. Governments are asked to "consider what unilateral steps for disarmament could responsibly be taken" (which is not a call for unilateral disarmament, however).[87]

When the theory of a just war is applied to revolution, ecumenical agreement breaks down. Catholic tradition knows of the possibility of a just revolution, but has been consistently reluctant to see this theory employed. In recent years Rome has stressed the inadmissibility of revolutionary violence, as if *this* kind of violence were substantially different from the sanctioned violence of a defensive war. Of course, just-war theory is careful, and not easily used to justify a given war; many Christians today are afraid of justifying contemporary violence too readily. Perhaps it is the very caution of the just-war theory that makes the Holy See wary of approving any war today. Whatever the cause, the Vatican tends to disapprove sternly of contemporary attempts to excuse violence. Even in the struggle for freedom from systematic oppression, "violence is always to be excluded." Justice comes not by violence, but by reform and the conversion of hearts, however gradual.[88]

This flat prohibition stands despite an admission that violence is already present from the side of the oppressors. Pope Paul referred to the "structural violence of some political regimes" even while condemning violence used against them. The repeated argument is that violence cannot ultimately serve justice or liberation, but ends by begetting more violence and leading to greater oppression. "As long as selective support is given to certain forms of violence in line with interests or ideologies . . . then . . . restraint will give way in the face of the simple and brutal logic of violence. . . ." The Roman Catholic Church does stand for "liberation of the poor, the oppressed, and the outcaste 'freed from servitude imposed . . . by other men.' " It also denies that the hope of the eschaton blunts its commitment "to offer people a definite approximation or anticipation of the new world" in this world. And yet it prefers, instead of a violent uprising to attain this liberation, that the victims of oppression should display "readiness to accept suffering, persecution, even death as Christ himself did."[89]

Although WCC grants to liberation movements may not be used for military purposes,[90] the World Council nevertheless is supporting movements engaged in guerrilla warfare, and its attitude toward violence is obviously not to condemn it in all situations. But neither is the WCC careless or callous about violence, and in fact it hedges the use of violence about with warnings and limitations:

> Some Christians will be among those who, despairing of the removal or reduction of economic injustice by peaceful means, feel obliged to have recourse to violence as a last resort. In such circumstances, both violent action and passive inaction come under God's judgment. Since recourse to violence could end in a defeat for both justice and order, special attention should be paid to non-violent strategies for the achievement of change.[91]

Speaking of Northern Ireland, the Executive Committee noted that "present problems cannot be resolved by violence or counter-violence and . . . a military solution is no solution."[92] Nonviolent solutions are always the desirable way, and World Council agencies are urged to work hard at finding constructive ways to use nonviolent action.[93]

At the same time, however, violence in an uprising must be understood in the context of the bloodshed caused by the regime in the first place, including such matters as "the constant destruction of lives carelessly caused by some structures of contemporary society such as inhumane working conditions." When a legitimate cause is repressed by the violence of the status quo, revolutionary counterviolence may be justifiable, despite its moral ambiguity.[94] The Central Committee states the vexing dilemma this way:

[The Central Committee] believes that the churches must always stand for the liberation of the oppressed and of victims of violent measures which deny basic human rights. It calls attention to the fact that violence is in many cases inherent in the maintenance of the status quo. Nevertheless the WCC does not and cannot identify itself completely with any political movement, nor does it pass judgment on those victims of racism who are driven to violence as the only way left to them to redress grievances and so open the way for a new and more just social order.[95]

This is the position subsequently taken in the World Council's careful study on the question of violence, which the Central Committee formally adopted in 1973. The report neither condemns nor supports violence, but discusses different types of force in different settings, noting disagreements on the issue. The emphasis is clearly on restraint: Violence is demonic; nonviolent strategies of change are much to be preferred. Some forms of violence, like torture and deliberately killing noncombatants, are always wrong and destructive to the souls of the perpetrators of such acts. But then, Christians do have an obligation to resist tyranny; the report—and the Central Committee that adopted it—do not pass judgment on those driven to violence as a last resort, nor will they turn their backs on them.[96]

So despite the fact that the World Council and the Holy See share the tradition of the just war, and share also the profound Christian reluctance to sanction the use of violence, they end up with very different judgments about the way that tradition should be applied to contemporary revolutionary movements for social justice. The Vatican has never openly sided with a national liberation movement, because in the first place that would be to bless publicly a political action; and in the second place, that would be to tolerate if not to endorse violence. The World Council, despite a clear reluctance to accept violent solutions, is readier to see the overthrow of an evil state, and willing to admit that the violence in an existing oppressive situation may admit of no other remedy than counterviolence.

Economic Development and Technology

In ecumenical work of recent years economic development has become a high-priority item, defended as virtually a necessary corollary of human rights. For both the World Council and the Roman Catholic Church, Christian solidarity with the poor must mean an active commitment to making the necessities of life available to all. Their work is not what "a mere welfare agency or a mere humanitarian enterprise" might do, but "is nourished by God's costly love as revealed in Jesus Christ. . . . All our service is a response to the God who first loved us. Justice is the expression of this love in the structure of society."[97] Christian responsibility must extend to the whole world and must be based on an ethic of solidarity, sharing, and mutual sacrifice. Individuals should not increase their own material wealth until the basic needs of all are satisfied; indeed, the consumption of the wealthy should be reduced. Said the assembled Catholic bishops:

> It is impossible to see what right the richer nations have to keep up their claim to increase their own material demands, if the consequence is either that others remain in misery or that the danger of destroying the very physical foundations of life on earth is precipitated.[98]

Likewise the World Council's Nairobi Assembly declared succinctly, "Nobody should increase his affluence until everybody has his essentials."[99] Economic development is a sign of a full human existence, "a responsible society in which man's freedom and dignity as a creature of God are fully respected." It must be participatory, a people's movement against oppression. Development is for the sake of the common good of humanity, a matter of greater justice in the distribution of the earth's goods.[100]

It is crucial for Christian action in development aid to go beyond simple charity. Charity does nothing to change the preponderance of wealth and power on one side, and it preserves the relation of dependence in which the poor find themselves. Development is a journey out of dependence toward liberation and self-reliance. It involves a primary shift of relations, a transfer of power, the economic analogue to the political process of decolonization. So it requires not simply the voluntary largesse of the comfortable but also structural changes in economic patterns to free the poor from begging. Ecumenical statements are full of ideas for promoting such changes. They include taxes on luxuries to create a world development fund; taxes (1 or 2 percent have been proposed) on gross national product as a form of world redistribution of wealth; changes in trading patterns and rules to promote equity, like stablilizing the prices of primary products; preferential market access for developing countries' exports; better debt terms and the rescheduling of burdensome debts owed by the less developed countries; encouragement of agriculture and labor-intensive industries rather than showcase prestige projects that benefit only a few; and, at least as a concept, the New International Economic Order proposal of the Third World countries at the United Nations.[101]

It is the ecumenical conviction that governments must be the primary factors in facilitating development, as they have so much more power and influence than private, nongovernmental agencies. Nevertheless the churches must play an exemplary role, committing themselves to the cause by serious and sacrificial programs. The organizational structures of both sides reflect the commitment. Both Caritas Internationalis and the Division of Interchurch Aid, Refugee and World Service have development emphases (particularly the WCC's Commission on the Churches' Participation in Development, within the larger division). And of course there is, or was, Sodepax itself, the joint project. Despite the ambiguity and precariousness of its position, Sodepax had development as a central concern, as shown by the Beirut conference with which its program began in 1968. Otherwise ecumenical cooperation is better seen at the local level; Action for Food Production (AFPRO) in India is one of the better-known and most dramatic examples.

Probably the principal reason why cooperation is best at the local level is that development projects are inevitably specific, and the Holy See's reluctance to commit itself to specific programs restrains its enthusiasm for pursuing joint global policies with the WCC. Local projects have the merit of being contained, formed by local conditions, and not susceptible to ideological interpretation. Situations differ around the world, and no one analysis or solution (notably Marxism) can be applied to all. Human development is not to be identified with the kingdom of God. "Prophetic charges of injustice and urgent appeals to make common cause with the poor have to do with situations that are highly complex in nature," said a papal theological commission, and cannot be settled by theology or ideology, nor, obviously, by the two in combination.[102]

One particular aspect of the development debate on which both the Roman Catholic Church and the World Council have independently taken a noteworthy position concerns the ownership and use of natural resources, including food. Both espouse the rather radically anti-nationalist view that all humanity must have access to the world's resources, which are the common heritage of the race. Those particular resources not yet claimed, like the seabed, should be used by all, especially for the benefit of the poorest. Such resources should not become the property solely of well-positioned states (as unfortunately the U.N. Law of the Sea Treaty would to a great extent permit). In a reversal of the customary roles, the Roman Catholic Church is even sharper and more detailed on this point than the World Council, perhaps because Rome tends historically to be more critical of the claims of national sovereignty. "The goods of the earth are destined primarily for universal use and for the subsistence of all men, before any individual appropriation." But both sides are alike in basing their judgments on the purpose of the Creator in giving the earth to all humankind collectively, so that sharing is an act of obedience to the divine purpose.[103]

The long and extensive history of ecumenical discussions on the economic order has tended to yield in recent years to this single issue of development. Although John Paul's encyclical on work speaks in the traditional way—once common also to the WCC—by even-handedly criticizing liberal capitalism for its antihuman orientation toward material production and socialism for a collectivism inimical to worker participation in property ownership, the traditional issues concerning economic systems are now viewed mainly through the development prism. An economic ordering of society, whether it be socialism or the free-market economy or whatever, tends to be judged by its capacity for raising the poor and narrowing the gap between them and the rich, not only among nations but within them. A just system must provide everyone with the means necessary to maintain life, spreading the economy's benefits to all. There is criticism of any order and institutions, including selfish labor unions (though the necessity for unions is still defended), that function so as to concentrate power and wealth at the expense of the good of all. There is an equalitarian bias that emphasizes the social responsibility of private property, particularly of land, whose ownership may be too narrowly based. One particular form of private economic activity, the multinational corporations, comes in for some sharp criticism, particularly from the World Council, which regards them as vehicles of neocolonialism.[104]

There is increasing discussion within the ecumenical bodies over the role to be played in development by technology. The dominant view in both the Roman Catholic Church and World Council is not hostile to technology, but regards it rather as a powerful tool of great potential, even while the threat of its misuse must be contained. "If authentic, Christian life will express joy and gratitude over the possibility to be co-workers with God in a creation stirred to newness by scientific and technical inventions," said the World Council's Uppsala Assembly.[105] In a similar vein the encyclical *Populorum Progressio* affirmed:

> Industry is a necessity for economic growth or human progress. . . . By persistent work and use of his intelligence man gradually wrests nature's secrets from her and finds a better application for her riches.[106]

Pope John Paul II has gone out of his way to express a positive attitude toward "objective" science and to cultivate the scientific community, even publically repenting the Galileo case and other examples of the Church's past obdurateness. This includes a cautiously revisionist appreciation of Pierre Teilhard de Chardin, whose works were censured by the Holy Office as recently as 1962. "We have no reason to regard our scientific and technological culture as inimical to the world of God's creation."[107]

Of course, this is not an uncritical adulation. There have been warnings, particularly in the most recent years, that an ill-considered use of technology entails the danger of environmental degradation and dehumanization, not only for the developed nations but also for traditional cultures. There is concern that land needed for food production will be lost. There is fear that science and technology will be put to ever more dangerous uses. And there is a reiteration of the traditional fear that some forms of industrial society promote the alienation of humanity from nature and from work.[108]

Nevertheless, technology represents an opportunity for the poor of the earth. Properly used, it will not hurt the human habitation, but improve it. Its value is in its potential contribution to development and hence to justice. The World Council especially, which has carried on an extensive study project on the uses and impact of science and technology culminating in an international conference at the Massachusetts Institute of Technology in 1979, has from the beginning linked its assessment to the question of social justice. It has stressed the need to overcome inequalities of power, to assure equal access to technology, and to make certain that these new devices and methods really do serve the poor.[109]

The ecumenical tendency to stress the positive uses of technology extends even to that most problematic of scientific developments, nuclear power. Here again the study work has been done mainly by the World Council; the Holy See for the most part simply echoes the conclusions of the WCC. There are, to be sure, contradictory tendencies in the WCC constituency, and some church groups in developed countries have mounted something of a holy war against nuclear energy. On the other side appear many representatives of poorer countries for whom nuclear technology is one of the keys to development, particularly if they lack other potential sources of energy. The World Council has generally sided with the latter group, refusing to condemn nuclear power. Acknowledging the great risks, especially radiation leakage from stored wastes and the diversion of atomic materials to weapons, the WCC statements have nonetheless argued for keeping the nuclear option open while work goes forward on making it safer, on developing alternative sources of energy, and on attempting to reduce energy consumption in the developed world so that the savings may be transferred to less developed areas. However, a note of uncertainty entered WCC policy when an unplanned motion from the floor at the 1980 Central Committee meeting resulted in a close vote (46–30, with 12 abstentions) favoring a five-year moratorium on the construction of new nuclear power plants pending an evaluation of their safety.

Of all the risks associated with nuclear power, it is a political one that most of all seems to disturb ecumenical reflection. According to this view, power will be ever more concentrated in the hands of the few nations who are technologically sophisticated and rich enough to deploy nuclear plants. Hence the World Council, even though it supports the nonproliferation treaty for nuclear weapons, and is well aware that the spread of nuclear technology is likely to lead to the spread of such weapons in spite of the treaty, nevertheless protests the exclusion of the nonnuclear nations from access to the requisite technology. Although this is a difficult and dangerous position, it is consistent with the World Council's concern to see the world's power imbalance redressed.[110]

Population, Women, and Family Issues

Of all the areas in social ethics, those that are most likely to produce extensive and substantive difference between the Holy See and the World Council concern population limitation and the role of women. Yet the differences are not manifested quite the way one might anticipate.

On the question of overpopulation, both sides view the matter with alarm, noting the connection between ever-rising numbers and ever-growing hunger. Both say that population pressure makes economic development much more difficult, often using up more than the annual rise in gross national product, so that a nation's standard of living shows a net decline. But of the two, the World Council is certainly ahead on this issue, both in the length of time it has been addressing the problem and in the frankness of its utterances:

> We recognize that even the most promising combination of measures for increased food production will only postpone catastrophe unless there is a vast increase in responsible family life and planning.
>
> The implications of the world's unprecedented population explosion are far-reaching with regard to long-range economic planning, the provision of food, employment, housing, education, and health services. Many churches are agreed that we need to promote family planning and birth control as a matter of urgency.[111]

The Holy See has come only lately, reluctantly, and half-heartedly to this cause. The right of parents to beget children is traditionally affirmed without qualification, a private right belonging to the autonomous sphere of the family. It was a new theme when *Populorum Progressio* suggested that parents should consider their responsibility to the community in procreation as part of the exercise of their "rightful" freedom, and that public authorities might intervene to encourage population limitation. But this theme has not really been taken up in subsequent official utterances. Even though the demographic problem is often alluded to, no truly meaningful encouragement is offered for its solution. Far from pursuing the allusion to a possible role for public authorities, the Vatican seems actually fearful of government interjection into the issue, raising the specter of forced population limitation, whether by a state on its own citizens, or by a state on other states as a condition of aid. Against this the Holy See insists on the unhindered, and perhaps even uninfluenced right of families to choose freely the number of their children. (The state should preferably even leave sex education to families.) Rome seems almost blind to the adverse economic consequences of rising population, simply insisting that states should make provision for them so that couples may have big families if they wish:

> It is impossible not to mention as a priority the right of parents to have children as they wish, receiving at the same time what is needed to educate them in dignity and the right bearing of life.[112]
> It is the positive duty of government to help bring about conditions that will relieve pressures on couples to limit family size.[113]

The calls to limit population for the sake of economic development, while they exist as noted, are oddly muted and qualified. The emphasis falls elsewhere, on development to provide for increasing numbers. Public policy should stress development and not population limitation. Pope Paul's famous declaration at the United Nations set the tone:

> You must strive to multiply bread . . . and not rather favor an artificial control of birth, which would be irrational, in order to diminish the number of guests at the banquet of life.[114]

Again:

> It is inadmissible that those who have control of the wealth and resources of mankind should try to resolve the problem of hunger by forbidding the poor to be

born. . . . Is it not a new form of warfare to impose a restrictive demographic policy on nations, to ensure that they will not claim their just share of the earth's goods?[115]

This logic obviously results in reducing *everyone's* "just share," a point acknowledged by the present pope, who, however, seems also to favor large families no matter what the economic consequences:

> It is certainly less serious to deny children certain comforts or material advantages than to deprive them of the presence of brothers and sisters who could help them to grow in humanity. . . .[116]

He is critical of exponents of limiting population as having "an anti-life mentality" because of

> a certain panic deriving from the studies of ecologists and futurologists on population growth, which sometimes exaggerate the danger of demographic increase to the quality of life. . . . Human life, even if weak and suffering, is always a splendid gift of God's goodness.[117]

However dangerous the Vatican position may be for the world's demographic problem, it does have the political utility of appealing to much Third World sentiment. John Paul's repeated celebration on his African trip of the African love of large families illustrates the point: Emerging nations often take pride in their growing population, want development to support their numbers, and suspect western calls for population control of being a way to limit their power. The Holy See has support for its position from many Third World bishops, while western prelates often squirm uncomfortably.

Of course, population limitation is inseparably tied to the

problem of contraception. It is surely here that one finds the real reason for the Vatican stance: an ethic of means that flatly prohibits most forms of contraception, no matter the consequences. Even if it is desirable to limit population, the most effective means for doing so are not licit. Paul VI's famous encyclical *Humanae Vitae* puts this judgment firmly and definitively: Excluded is "direct interruption of the generative process already begun," and "direct sterilization, whether perpetual or temporary," and:

> every action which, either in anticipation of the conjugal act, or in its accomplishment, or in the development of its natural consequences, proposes . . . to render procreation impossible.[118]

This decision is based on a reading of natural law, "the eternal norms of natural ethics," as "the laws that God has impressed on the body and spirit of man," meaning, apparently, that "nature's way" is to be understood as the will of God. This is why the so-called rhythm method of birth control is acceptable, and why the popes call for research to make "natural methods" like this more effective because it "respects the order established by God" in making "legitimate use of natural disposition." Vatican statements can be positive about the planned spacing of children and even about the uses of sexuality for purposes other than procreation, to "strengthen marital communication" (although "virginity or celibacy [is still] the supreme form . . . of human sexuality"). But the "contraceptive mentality" is denounced as against the primary purpose of marriage, which is to beget children. This fundamental intention of the divine plan cannot be permanently denied, and not even temporarily thwarted if that is accomplished by "unnatural means."[119]

So firm is this conviction that the teaching of *Humanae Vitae* has been repeatedly and bluntly reaffirmed by the

Holy See in the teeth of persistent widespread opposition to it. Couples distressed by it are simply called to discipline and obedience. It is to be obeyed *now,* not held merely as a goal to strive for; the sacrifice entailed is good for one's spiritual development. Contraception by "artificial" means is linked with abortion as a deadly attack on the right to life, and no yielding on this issue is possible. This immovable attitude and the realization that the dreaded illicit means will be and are being encouraged by secular authorities stand as barriers to the participation of Rome in campaigns to limit births.[120]

Not surprisingly, then, it has always been difficult to discuss this question in ecumenical meetings. However, the divisions and tensions are not only between the two sides but within them. Contraception as well as the larger demographic problems and the role of women are issues between the Vatican and Catholic laity and clergy as much as an ecumenical controversy. As with population control, opposition to the official stance is greatest among Catholics in developed countries. Those from developing countries are more likely to favor *Humanae Vitae* as a defense of poor people, with antiwestern implications—although with individual couples anywhere the problem is likely to be real and difficult.

The World Council's constituency is also badly divided on these issues. The Orthodox are often particularly set apart, so that the WCC's official statements are reluctant to go beyond pointing to the problem. Instead, the World Council's characteristic formula is employed: "Some say . . . while others say." "Some churches may have moral objections to certain methods of population control," and family planning must be by means "acceptable in conscience to parents." As with the Roman Catholic Church, the rich/poor disparity is also part of the problem. The World Council maintains that population control must not be seen as a substitute for economic development, even while it deplores the effect of population increase on that development. Its fear is that western nations (or perhaps one should say now "northern nations") may use population growth in poor countries as an excuse not to give them development assistance on the grounds that their situation is hopeless.[121]

Something of the same pattern is evident in the matter of abortion, where the insistent Roman Catholic attack on the procedure[122] meets largely silence from the WCC because of the latter's divided constituency. The subject has been discussed in study conferences, but tends to be avoided at higher levels of pronouncement. One may expect similar ambiguity as some of the newer issues in medical ethics reach the highest levels of ecumenical discussion, that is, that divisions within either or both sides will blunt the potential divisiveness of these subjects *between* the Roman Catholic Church and the WCC. The Vatican Congregation for the Doctrine of the Faith has already issued detailed rules governing the treatment of terminally ill patients, and Pope John Paul has warned doctors against excessive technological intervention.[123] But these are fearsomely complex subjects on which hardened, polarized positions are unlikely to develop.

The World Council has paid more attention than the Holy See in recent years to the feminist issue, declaring rather roundly for equal status for women and their full participation in social, economic, and political life. Spurred on by its own subunit on Women in Church and Society, a symbolically important specialized program maintained in the face of budgetary pressures to drop it, the World Council's language has become increasingly visionary: ". . . a new humanity in which women would enjoy a new liberation and freedom, involving responsibility, love for others, and a place in decision making."[124]

The goal of liberation for equality and full humanity, deliberately invoking words in which the World Council speaks of the poor and oppressed, does not exclude the

Church itself, nor spare it criticism. Women have been excluded from full leadership roles in the churches, as in society at large. The very language of the Church, even in worship, has at times seemed to exclude them; and the World Council has made a start on eliminating what it calls, adopting the terminology of the feminist movement, "sexist language" ("chairman," "spokesman"). Unfortunately any serious attempt at equality of roles in the Church bumps into the thorny question of women's ordination, which is resisted stoutly by the Orthodox and some Anglicans. The World Council is far from resolving this issue, which indeed seems at an impasse. It is significant, however, that it has been insistently raised in WCC meetings, forcing statements on the subject, even if the wording has to be negotiated with the Orthodox. Meanwhile, the World Council has pressed the issue of women's roles in the Church on another front, by resolving rather dramatically to move to equal participation of women and men on all of its own decision-making and advisory bodies—again, over considerable Orthodox uneasiness. Plainly, divisive though the feminist issue may be, and fraught with difficult doctrinal questions, it is a subject formally and regularly addressed in the WCC, not ignored.[125]

For the only slightly less sensitive area of family structure the World Council opts for a certain ambivalence, keeping one foot firmly in tradition while acknowledging the force of change. "We believe that physical intercourse, personal commitment, and marriage form a dynamic unity." But the increasing plurality of family styles must at least be recognized as a subject for study; and the organization of even the traditional monogamous unit ought to move toward more mutuality, toward equal sharing of family responsibilities.[126]

The Roman Catholic Church bears a tradition more reluctant to challenge traditional sex-role distinctions. There has been historically a strong emphasis on the rights and autonomy of the family against more complex forms of social organization like the state; and within the family, the special and distinct role of women is regularly cited with approval. When, under the pressure of the women's movement, the Vatican does in fact declare itself for "equality with men to participate in the educational, cultural, economic, social, and political life of the state," one looks for and finds the traditional balancing note, the importance at the same time of "protect[ing] woman's role as mother, responsible for the home and the font of life":

> We do not have in mind that false equality which would deny the distinctions laid down by the Creator himself and which would be in contradiction with woman's proper role . . . at the heart of the family as well as within society.

This is a position that speaks of equality, but makes it clear that women have a primary role in the family that must not be lost, no matter what they may aspire to accomplish in public life. In that their vocation is certainly different from men's. Vatican documents often present themselves as the defender of women by saying that women ought not to be forced for economic reasons to work outside the home; but the pronouncements do not really speak to or for women who *wish* to work outside the home. Economic life should be so ordered that "women not be forced to engage in external work, . . . but rather so that the family might be able to live rightly, that the mother might devote herself fully to the family." Women should not "have to pay for their advancement by abandoning what is specific to them and at the expense of the family, in which women as mothers have an irreplaceable role." Women should not be honored more for their work outside the home than for their work in it. The ideal of women's equality would be served by raising the value attributed by society to women's work in the home.

Indeed, the different vocations of men and women are presented as in the eternal plan of the Creator, based on created differences between the sexes, even to fundamental sex-linked personality differences:

> It is clear that if man is by temperament more inclined to deal with exterior affairs, public activities, woman has, generally speaking, greater insight and finer tact to know and solve the delicate problems of domestic and family life, the basis of all social life; which does not prevent some women from showing great skill in every field of public activity.

Woman has typically "devotion, sweetness, and refinement," "intuition, creativity, sensibility, a sense of piety and compassion, a profound capacity for understanding and love"—qualities particularly suited for use within the family. Traditional role distinctions are thus kept, while an attempt is made to eliminate the harmful effects of these distinctions. Offenses against the dignity of women are decried, but the proper response of man to woman is quite literally paternalistic: Husbands are to show "charity both gentle and strong" toward their wives, like Christ's love for the church, and fathers are to "reveal and relive on earth the very fatherhood of God."[127]

All in all, despite formal bows in the direction of public equality for the sexes, this is a more conserving, traditional, and defensive vision of women's place than that so often heard in the World Council.

The role of women within the Church is a particularly sensitive and contentious issue among Catholics today. It has been examined and discussed at the level of study commissions and individual scholars, who have sometimes found the question of ordination potentially open:

> The masculine character of the hierarchical order which has structured the church since its beginning

> seems attested to by scripture in an undeniable way.
> Must we conclude that this rule must be valid forever
> in the church? . . . Is it possible that certain circum-
> stances can come about which call on the church to
> entrust to certain women some sacramental minis-
> tries? This has been the case with baptism. . . . Is it
> possible that we will come to this even with the minis-
> try of eucharist and reconciliation. . . ?

But at the official level, ordination for women is foreclosed,
and the possibility seems very distant. The formal position
of the Holy See is:

> the fact of conferring priestly ordination only on men,
> . . . [a] norm based on Christ's example, has been and
> is still observed because it is considered to conform to
> God's plan for his church.[128]

The restiveness of Catholic women may eventually lead—or
push—the hierarchy in new directions; but for the present
the combination of official conservatism and internal tension makes the Roman Catholic Church an unlikely partner
for ecumenical dialogue on the role of women.

The Holy See spends much more time on family issues
than the World Council does. Topics like marriage and
divorce are extensively treated and repeatedly the subject of
official teaching. The traditional view of the family—
monogamous, indissoluble, with life-long fidelity—is
stoutly defended against all the eroding forces of contemporary society, economic, political, sociological, and psychological. Even cultural relativity is no excuse for devia-
tion: Conjugal communion "is radically contradicted by
polygamy." The family's autonomy must be defended
against state interference, while at the same time the state is
obliged to insure that families receive adequate economic
support, health care, education, and housing. Sexual rela-

tions belong only to marriage. Trial marriages, free unions, and even merely civil marriages for Catholics are denounced; Catholic couples are not to be admitted to the sacraments until they marry properly within the Church. In religiously mixed marriages the Catholic partner has the obligation to raise the children as Catholics, though no "undue pressure" should be put on the other partner to change. Divorce can under no circumstances be sanctioned, nor remarriage after civil divorce. Even abandoned spouses must be encouraged to "preserve their fidelity even in their difficult situation." Catholics who do have civil divorces and remarriages should not be separated from the Church, but cannot be admitted to the Eucharist unless they break off their second marriage, or if that is not possible, unless they live celibately in that illicit union.[129]

For all this detail there is simply no matching WCC documentation, as the work of the Family Ministries Department does not often reach the level of a Central Committee or Assembly declaration. It is hard for the WCC, at that level, to reach a consensus on family and sexual issues. What there is is considerably less confident and certain in tone than the Vatican's speech, which reads like embattled conviction defending an endangered traditionalism against the corrosions of the modern world. The WCC is far more tentative; and at present a developed, defined difference between the two bodies seems unlikely.

Chapter 4

CONCLUSIONS: WHAT HOPE FOR THE FUTURE?

Effective cooperation on social issues between the Roman Catholic Church and the World Council of Churches would be as useful as it would be remarkable. In a volatile and dangerous world these religious bodies with their subtle but strong influence, their excellent sources of information, their worldwide networks, and their detachment from the politics of nation-states are superbly positioned to be mediators of conflicts and promoters of the universal good of humankind. Their potential for disinterested benevolence could, if realized, enable them to save victims of human-rights violations, defuse quarrels that lead to wars, facilitate the transfer of people and goods among nations according to need, and develop an active awareness of the unity of the human race that transcends national parochialism and lays an ideological foundation for effective agencies of international cooperation.

All this could happen, and to a very limited extent it already does. But the successes are woefully few and irregular, the potential mostly unrealized, the opportunities mainly lost. Of course, unity at the summit for joint action would be far more likely if the putative partners were each more internally unified. Instead, conditions of tension and sometimes downright disarray lead to uncertainty, insecurity, and hesitation in addressing the world. This situation is most obvious in the case of the World Council, despite the boldness of its speech on some issues; for here different traditions lie together in a loose voluntary alliance whose agencies depend on a rough consensus to act. Sometimes it seems as if all the complications possible to Christendom are brought under one roof, making a bedlam of doctrines and rites and cultures and social policies. To be sure, there are those—professional optimists and bureaucrats whose job is to minimize differences and present harmony to the world—who prefer to emphasize the unity of WCC thought rather than the reverse. A tradition does exist, with continuity, as the preceding pages show. But it is largely a unity of accidents, or more precisely of coincidences, where the diversity within the World Council happens to coalesce around certain issues—racism, for example, hence the possibility of an action program; or the fragile agreement on violence; or development; or religious liberty; or, potentially at least, technology. Someone has called such issues "islands of consensus" within a great sea of differences where no effective common action is possible. Not even the doctrinal foundations of social witness are agreed upon.

If internal differences manifestly belong to the very nature of the WCC, the fissures within the Roman Catholic Church are less obvious, and usually treated as signs of trouble rather than being in the nature of the body. Yet quite aside from the tensions peculiar to the post-Vatican II era, which were discussed here earlier, the Church spans so many different cultures and includes such a diversity of peoples that not even its centralized administration and its theology of authority can eliminate the restraints on action posed by the threat of division. Always the Holy See must beware of offending the faithful, always sense the limits beyond which it moves at peril of disruption. Even that most impressive symbol of Roman Catholic unity, the papacy, is bound by the limits that follow from its visibility. The pope is a massive public event whose words and actions are reported worldwide and scrutinized for subtle shades of meaning. What he says and does in one context will be applied to other contexts, and he must always be aware of that and couch his remarks in broad terms. The need to speak universally always threatens to reduce his utterances to impotent generalities. He must be careful about risking the prestige of his office, and even his person must be closely guarded. He is really a sort of prisoner of his position and must live and move and have his being within its historic boundaries—which fact, of course, limits his capacity to act in the world. In short, the Vatican is not as solid or powerful sociologically and politically as it may appear to be, and it could use allies.

Seeing the possibilities and sensing their mutual need, the Holy See and the World Council have certainly *talked* common witness. And even though they have little to show for it so far, some promising areas have appeared. Development, the arms race, and, in theory at least, human rights, including religious liberty and the elimination of racism and torture, are all topics where agreement is real and some concerted action may be possible. Sodepax is dead, but it has been replaced by a new collaborative arrangement established by the Joint Working Group in November 1980 to do common research and reflection on social questions. More recently, in September 1981, the parent bodies established a new Joint Consultative Group on Social Thought and Action (JCG). Whether this new arrangement will succeed where Sodepax did not remains to be seen. One may be permitted some pessimism, given the fate of Sodepax. But at least the JCG proposes to begin positively by developing common Roman Catholic-World Council statements on torture and the arms race, to publish a joint booklet on threats to peace, and to deal collaboratively with church aid and relief, social action education, and the problem of ethical method.[130] As common statements have hitherto proved virtually impossible to produce, even a serious proposal to make them may be accounted progress.

That said, one returns to the barriers with renewed respect for their persistent power. It is not simply the substantive disagreement on some issues—violence, sex and family matters, the relation of the local (e.g., nations) to the universal—but the very way of doing public ethics, the conception of the proper function of the Church, the essential nature of the two bodies. There is a fundamental dissymmetry at work. Some in the Joint Working Group who first heard this essay thought that it criticized the behavior of both sides with an eye to spurring them to change. But the problem lies in basic forces that are just *reflected* in personalities, and only to a much lesser degree in the personalities themselves. These forces are not amenable to alteration by simple fiat. It would be wrong to read this work as a catalogue of complaints about human folly in the face of the manifest value of ecumenical cooperation. We confront here tendencies built into the Roman Catholic Church and the World Council of Churches, ways of behaving almost inexorably pushing the would-be partners apart. Reversal, if it happens, will require more than good intentions. Many more basic changes must first appear; perhaps most important, if one were to guess, a spreading experience of ecumenical cooperation at the local level. Common declarations at the summit are likely to lag behind common action in communities. The more is the pity, for effective unity at the top might inspire, and not just follow, united Christian social witness on the field.

NOTES

1. See the posthumous report of Franklin Clark Fry to the Uppsala Assembly, *The Uppsala Report 1968: Official Report of the Fourth Assembly of the World Council of Churches, Uppsala, July 4-20, 1968,* ed. Norman Goodall (Geneva: World Council of Churches, 1968), p. 279. Cf. speech of Roberto Tucci at Uppsala, ibid. pp. 323-33.

2. Ibid., p. 221.

3. *Minutes of the Executive Committee of the World Council of Churches,* February 1970, pp. 8-9; *Minutes, Executive Committee,* August-September 1970, p. 7; *Minutes of the Central Committee of the World Council of Churches,* 1971, pp. 36-37.

4. *Minutes, Central Committee,* 1971, pp. 41, 42.

5. Ibid.

6. *Minutes, Central Committee,* 1967, pp. 53, 146.

7. *Minutes, Executive Committee,* February 1972, pp. 6, 22, 23.

8. "Evangelization of the Modern World," Synod of Bishops, 26 October 1974, in Joseph Gremillion, ed., *The Gospel of Peace and Justice: Catholic Social Teaching since Pope John* (Maryknoll, N.Y.: Orbis Books, 1976), p. 596; *Evangelii Nuntiandi* 77; John Paul II, speech in Sistine Chapel, 17 October 1978, *Origins* 8:293, cf. pp. 307-8; *Redemptor Hominis* 6; John Paul II, address in Istanbul, 30 November 1979, *Origins* 9:415, 422-27 passim; John Paul II, address to German bishops at Fulda, 17 November 1980, *Origins* 10:387; John Paul II, address to the Council of the Evangelical Church in Germany, Mainz, 17 November 1980, ibid., pp. 398-99; John Paul II, telegram to the Joint Working Group, Le Louverain, Neuchâtel, March 1979; John Paul II, address to Jesuits, Rome, 27 February 1982, *Origins* 11:627.

9. *Redemptor Hominis* 6; *Catechesi Tradendae* 32. Cf. Paul VI, "Bull of Indication of the Holy Year 1975," Gremillion, ed., pp. 584-85; Paul VI, last will, *Origins* 8:176; John Paul I, address to cardinals and the world, 27 August 1978, *Origins* 8:180; John Paul II, speech in Sistine Chapel, 17 October 1978, ibid., p. 293, cf. pp. 307-8; John Paul II, address to U.S. bishops, Chicago, 5 October 1979, *Origins* 9:290; John Paul II, address to cardinals and curia, 28 June 1980, *Origins* 10:170-72; John Paul II, address to lay church workers, 18 November 1980, Fulda, West Germany, ibid., p. 393; John Paul II, remarks to a working group

of the Faith and Order Commission of the World Council of Churches on baptism, eucharist, and the ministry, 3 November 1980, *Ecumenical Review* 33:83.

10. *Sapientia Christiana* 39; John Paul II, address to the plenary assembly of the Vatican Secretariat for Christian Unity, 8 February 1980, *Origins* 9:620. See also John Paul II, address to the Secretariat for Christian Unity, 18 November 1978, *Origins* 8:397–99; John Paul II, address to U.S. bishops, Chicago, 5 October 1979, *Origins* 9:290; John Paul II, address at Catholic University of America, 6 October 1979, ibid. pp. 307–8; John Paul II, address to the International Theological Commission, 26 October 1979, ibid., p. 394; declaration of the Vatican Sacred Congregation for the Doctrine of the Faith, 18 December 1979 on the Küng case, ibid., pp. 463, 465; John Paul II, letter to the German bishops on the Küng case, 15 May 1980, *Origins* 10:39–41; John Paul II, address to French bishops, Paris, 1 June 1980, ibid., p. 51; Philip Potter, general secretary of the World Council of Churches, on the Küng case, *Ecumenical Review* 32:192; letter from the Holy See through Pio Laghi, apostolic delegate to the United States, to U.S. bishops, and reply by the president and executive director of the Catholic Press Association, *Origins* 11:78–79; John Paul II, address to Jesuits, Rome, 27 February 1982, ibid., pp. 624–28.

11. *Minutes, Central Committee,* 1972, pp. 133–37, 141, 215–19, 58–60; *Minutes, Central Committee,* 1973, pp. 43, 75–78, 219; *Minutes, Central Committee,* 1974, pp. 20–21; *Breaking Barriers: Nairobi 1975. The Official Report of the Fifth Assembly of the World Council of Churches, Nairobi, 23 November–10 December 1975,* ed. David M. Paton (London: SPCK, and Grand Rapids, Mich.: Wm. B. Eerdmans Publishing Co., 1976), pp. 153–55, 199–201, 203, 205–6, 209, 228, 276–77; *Minutes, Central Committee,* 1976, p. 23; *Minutes, Central Committee,* 1979, pp. 28–30, 52–53; John Paul II, letter to the Joint Working Group, Neuchâtel, 23 February 1979.

12. "Justice in the World," Synod of Bishops 1971, Gremillion, ed., pp. 525–26.

13. Address to ecumenical leaders, Washington, D.C., 7 October 1979, *Origins* 9:295.

14. *Uppsala Report,* p. 493.

15. Ibid., p. 221.

16. See the comments of the structure study committee, *Minutes, Central Committee,* 1971, p. 159, and the mandate of Unit I (Faith and Witness), ibid., p. 162; *Minutes, Central Committee,* 1979, p. 16.

17. *Minutes, Central Committee,* 1969, p. 130, a perennial request; see also *Minutes, Central Committee,* 1976, p. 98.

18. And so Thomas defended it at Nairobi, *Nairobi Report,* p. 237.

19. *Humanae Vitae* 4.

20. For example, see *Minutes, Central Committee,* 1979, p. 17, mixed reactions to the "Just, Participatory, and Sustainable Society" study.

21. *Octogesima Adveniens* 4, 25, 26, 27, 28, 31, 35, 42, 45, 49, 50.

22. *Minutes, Central Committee,* 1972, pp. 46–47, 169–73; *Minutes, Central Committee,* 1974, pp. 31–32; *Nairobi Report,* pp. 81–82.

23. E.g., John Paul II, address to the Third General Assembly of Latin American bishops at Puebla, Mexico, 28 January 1979, III 2, 3; John Paul II, address to nuns in Mexico City, 27 January 1979, *Origins* 8:547; *Catechesi Tradendae* 52.

24. *Octogesima Adveniens* 26, 32–34; Paul VI, address to diplomats accredited to the Holy See, *Origins* 7:501–2; John Paul II, address to the Organization of American States, Washington, 6 October 1979, *Origins* 9:304; John Paul II, address to students at the University of Kinshasa, 4 May 1980, *Origins* 10:26; John Paul II, speech to diplomats at Nairobi, 6 May 1980, ibid., p. 31; John Paul II, address at St. Denis, Paris, 31 May 1980, ibid., p. 58; John Paul II to German and Italian scholars, Rome, 12 November 1981, *Origins* 11:379; John Paul II, World Day of Peace message, 21 December 1981, ibid., p. 474.

25. *Evangelii Nuntiandi* 27, 28; John Paul II, address at Puebla, 28 January 1979, I 4, 8, III 2, 3, 6 (in part quoting John Paul I and *Evangelii Nuntiandi*); *Redemptor Hominis* 13; John Paul II, homily in Nairobi, 7 May 1980, *Origins* 10:27; John Paul II in Rio de Janeiro, 2 July 1980, ibid., p. 124.

26. John Paul II, letter to all priests, 9 April 1979, *Origins* 8:696–704; John Paul II, address to Polish government officials, 2 June 1979, *Origins* 9:53; John Paul II, speech at the Shrine of the Immaculate Conception, Washington, 7 October 1979, ibid., pp. 284, 286 (the speech that drew the immediate and shocking public rejoinder from Sr. Theresa Kane of the Leadership Conference of Women Religious, calling for women's ordination); John Paul II, homily to members of the International Union of Superiors General, 14 November 1979, ibid., p. 410; John Paul II, speech to Zairean priests, 4 May 1980, *Origins* 10:11; John Paul II, speech to Brazilian bishops, Fortaleza, 10 July 1980, ibid., p. 136; John Paul II, address at ordination of priests, Rio de Janeiro, 2 July 1980, ibid., pp. 142–44; letter to dioceses and religious communities from the Vatican Congregation for the Doctrine of the Faith, 1980, ibid., pp. 335–36; John Paul II to Filipino priests, Manila, 17 February 1981, ibid., p. 589; John Paul II, radio message from Manila to Asian peoples, 21 February 1981, ibid., pp. 612–13; John Paul II, message to Chinese Christians, from Manila, 18 February 1981, ibid., p. 614.

27. "Justice in the World" (1971 synod of bishops), in Gremillion, ed., pp. 520–21; "Evangelization of the Modern World" (1974 Synod of Bishops), ibid., p. 597; *Evangelii Nuntiandi* 27–35; John Paul II in a general audience, 21 February 1979, *Origins* 8:600–601; *Laborem Exercens* 27, quoting *Gaudium et Spes* in part.

28. *Nairobi Report,* pp. 45, 63, 136, 233–35, 238–39; *Minutes, Central Committee,* 1979, pp. 16, 42–43; *Ecumenical Review* 30:278–80; *Ecumenical Review* 32:385.

29. John Paul II, World Day of Peace Message, 18 December 1979, *Origins* 9:459. Cf. his defense of these methods in his annual address to cardinals and curia, 22 December 1980, *Origins* 10:490–94.

30. *Minutes, Central Committee,* 1969, p. 142.

31. John Paul II, speech in Sistine Chapel, 17 October 1978, *Origins* 8:293; John Paul II, address to diplomats accredited to the Holy See, 20 October 1978, ibid., pp. 310–11; John Paul II, address to nuns in Mexico City, 27 January 1979, ibid., p. 547; John Paul II, address to priests, Mexico City, 27 January 1979, ibid., pp. 548–49; John Paul II, address to priests, Kinshasa, Zaire, 4 May 1980, *Origins* 10:11; John Paul II, homily in Nairobi, 7 May 1980, ibid., p. 27; John Paul II, address to Brazilian bishops, Fortaleza, 10 July 1980, ibid., p. 135; John Paul II, address at ordination of priests, Rio de Janeiro, 2 July 1980, ibid., pp. 142–44. Cf. directive from the Vatican Congregation for Religious and Secular Institutes, January 1981, ibid., p. 535; "Justice in the World," Gremillion, ed., p. 521; John Paul II, address to Nigerian priests and seminarians, Enugu, 13 February 1982, *Origins* 11:593; John Paul II, address to Jesuits, Rome, 27 February 1982, ibid., p. 627; statement from the Vatican's Clergy Congregation, confirmed by the pope, 8 March 1982, ibid., pp. 645, 647. Some directives against priests in politics may be aimed at local situations and catch others in other countries who are not the primary targets. The policy is, nevertheless, meant to be for the whole Church, universally applied.

32. Paul VI, World Day of Peace Message, January 1978, *Origins* 7:457; Paul VI, speech at Castelgondolfo, 16 July 1978, *Origins* 8:143–44; John Paul I, ibid., p. 272; John Paul II, address to the United Nations General Assembly, 2 October 1979, *Origins* 9:261; John Paul II, speech at Drogheda, Ireland, 29 September 1979, ibid., pp. 272–75; John Paul II, address to youth at Galway, Ireland, 30 September 1979, ibid., p. 276; John Paul II, speech to cardinals, 22 December 1979, ibid., p. 500; John Paul II, address to diplomats accredited to the Holy See, 14 January 1980, ibid., p. 571; John Paul II, speech to diplomats, Nairobi, 6 May 1980, *Origins* 10:31; John Paul II, speech to Philippine people, 17 February 1981, ibid., p. 591; John Paul II, public remarks on the Italian abortion referendum, *Origins* 11:2; statement of the Vatican delegate, Msgr. Mario Peressin, to the International Atomic Energy Agency, Vienna, 22 September 1981, ibid., p. 266.

33. Telegram of John Paul II, *Origins* 9:669; WCC message from Philip Potter, general secretary, 28 March 1980, *Ecumenical Review* 32:324; WCC Central Committee, 1980, in ibid., p. 431; Executive Committee, February 1981, in *Ecumenical Review* 33:189; John Paul II, remarks in Rome, 28 February 1982, *Origins* 11:615, 617; John Paul II, remarks in Rome, 7 March 1982, ibid., p. 630.

34. John Paul II, *Origins* 11:246; John Paul II, ibid., p. 518; John Paul II, address to diplomats accredited to the Vatican, 16 January 1982, ibid., pp. 561–62.

35. Constitution of the World Council of Churches, article IV, and Rule IX.

36. Rule X, 2; *Uppsala Report*, p. 480.

37. Rule X, 3, 4, 5; *Uppsala Report*, pp. 480–81.

38. *Uppsala Report*, p. 499.

39. For a good short discussion of the Holy See's unique status in international law, see Lukas Vischer, "The Holy See, the Vatican State, and the Churches' Common Witness: A Neglected Ecumenical Problem," *Journal of Ecumenical Studies* 11, no. 4 (1974): 617–35.

40. Paul VI, address to the United Nations General Assembly, 4 October 1965, Gremillion, ed., p. 380; John Paul I, address to diplomats accredited to the Vatican, 31 August 1978, *Origins* 8:198–99; John Paul II, address to the United Nations General Assembly, 2 October 1979, *Origins* 9:257, 259; John Paul II to the Executive Council of UNESCO, Paris, 2 June 1980, *Origins* 10:61.

41. This complaint is actually formally voiced in the *Nairobi Report,* p. 200, and it is very commonly expressed in private conversation.

42. *Minutes, Central Committee,* 1976, p. 39; *Minutes, Central Committee,* 1977, pp. 34–35; *Minutes, Central Committee,* 1979, pp. 28–30, 52–53.

43. See "The Primacy of Spiritual Values in the Advancement of Justice," address of Pope Paul VI to the Commission Justice and Peace, December 1977; also "Motu Proprio of Pope Paul VI Iustitiam et Pacem," 10 December 1976.

44. *Minutes, Executive Committee,* September 1971, p. 47; report of the Structure Committee, *Minutes, Central Committee,* 1971, pp. 182–83.

45. Pontifical Commission Justice and Peace, *The Church and Human Rights,* Vatican City 1975, p. 11, para. 14. Cf. ibid., pp. 6–7, paras. 3–6; p. 21, paras. 34, 35; pp. 21–22, paras. 36, 37; pp. 28–29, paras. 39, 40; p. 31, para. 43; pp. 32 ff. This document quotes from and summarizes current Catholic social teaching on human rights. Cf. also John Paul II, *Redemptor Hominis* 17; World Day of Peace Message, 8 December 1980, *Origins* 10:465, 467–70.

46. *The Church and Human Rights,* p. 37, para. 55.

47. Ibid., p. 24, para. 38; p. 8, para. 9; pp. 22–23, para. 37; pp. 63–64, para. 108; p. 25, para. 38 no. 9; *Justice in the World,* Gremillion, ed., pp. 525–26; Maurice Cardinal Roy, "Reflections on the Occasion of the Tenth Anniversary of the Encyclical *Pacem in Terris* of Pope John XXIII," 11 April 1973, Gremillion, ed., pp. 552–53; Paul VI, *Dignitatis Humanae* 6; letter of the Pontifical Commission for the Pastoral Care of Migrant and Itinerant Peoples, 26 May 1978, *Origins* 8:62; Paul VI, address to diplomats accredited to the Holy See, 14 January 1978, *Origins* 7:503; Paul VI, speech at Castelgandolfo, 16 July 1978, *Origins* 8:143; John Paul, message to United Nations Secretary General Kurt Waldheim on the 30th anniversary of the Universal Declaration of Human Rights, 11 December 1978, ibid., pp. 417, 419–20; interven-

tion of the Vatican delegate, Bishop Edouard Gagnon, at Habitat, the United Nations Conference on Human Settlements, 2 June 1976, *Origins* 6:79–80; John Paul II, address at Puebla, 28 January 1979, III.5; John Paul II, speech to workers in Guadalajara, 30 January 1979, *Origins* 8:559–60; John Paul II, homily at Birkenau (Auschwitz II), 7 June 1979, *Origins* 9:73–74; John Paul II, address to the United Nations General Assembly, 20 October 1979, ibid., pp. 259–60 and passim; John Paul II, address to the Organization of American States, Washington, 6 October 1979, ibid., p. 304; John Paul II, speech to cardinals, 27 December 1979, ibid., pp. 500–2; John Paul II, speech to Executive Council of UNESCO, Paris, 2 June 1980, *Origins* 10:59–60; John Paul II, remarks before the president of Brazil, Brasilia, 30 June 1980, ibid., p. 128; *Dives in Misericordia,* 11; *Laborem Exercens* 22, 23; John Paul II, address to diplomats accredited to the Vatican, 16 January 1982, *Origins* 11:562.

48. *The Church and Human Rights,* p. 23, para. 36, no. 8.

49. "Message to the People of God, from the World Synod of Bishops," 29 October 1977, Origins 7:321, 323–28. Cf. address of Pope Paul VI to diplomats accredited to the Holy See, 14 January 1978, *Origins* 7:503.

50. *The Church and Human Rights,* pp. 66–67, para. 116. See also Paul VI, address to the U.N. General Assembly, 21 October 1965, Gremillion, ed., p. 385; *Justice in the World,* Gremillion, ed., pp. 518–19; *Evangelii Nuntiandi* 39; Paul VI, speech at the end of the 1972 bishops' synod, *Origins* 7:351–52; synod of 1972, "Message to the People of God," ibid., p. 324; Paul VI, address to cardinals and curia, 5 January 1978, ibid., p. 457; Paul VI, address to diplomats accredited to the Holy See, 14 January 1978, ibid., pp. 501–2; John Paul II, message on the 30th anniversary of the Universal Declaration of Human Rights, *Origins* 8:420; *Redemptor Hominis* 12, 17; John Paul II, address to Polish bishops at Czestochowa, Poland, 5 June 1979, *Origins* 9:69–70; John Paul II, address to U.N. General Assembly, 2 October 1979, ibid., p. 265; *Catechesi Tradendae* 14; John Paul II, speech to cardinals, 22 December 1979, ibid., p. 502; John Paul II, remarks to the president of the Congo, Brazzaville, 5 May 1980, *Origins* 10:19; John Paul II, speech to diplomats, Nairobi, 6 May 1980, ibid., p. 31; John Paul II, speech to the Executive Council of UNESCO, Paris, ibid., p. 63; John Paul II, radio message from Manila to the Asian peoples, 21 February 1981, ibid., pp. 612–13; John Paul II, Christmas message, 25 December 1981, *Origins* 11:483.

51. *Uppsala Report,* p. 63; *Minutes, Central Committee,* 1971, pp. 269–76, 66–69; Sodepax, *Church Alert,* no. 18, pp. 18–19; *Minutes, Executive Committee,* September 1971, p. 37; *Minutes, Central Committee,* 1972, pp. 148–49; *Nairobi Report,* pp. 103, 104; *Minutes, Central Committee,* 1977, pp. 39–42.

52. *Uppsala Report,* p. 64. Cf. *Nairobi Report,* pp. 102–5.

53. *Minutes, Central Committee,* 1973, pp. 211–12.

54. *Minutes, Executive Committee,* February 1968, pp. 21–22; *Minutes, Central Committee,* 1971, pp. 68–69; *Uppsala Report,* p. 64; *Church Alert,* no. 18, pp. 18–19; *Nairobi Report,* pp. 103–5, 252–53, 307–8; *Minutes, Central Committee,* 1977, p. 39; *Minutes, Central Committee,* 1979, pp. 65–66; Executive Committee, February 1981, on the rights of the handicapped, *Ecumenical Review* 33:188.

55. *Uppsala Report,* pp. 64, 187; *Minutes, Central Committee,* 1967, pp. 47, 146; *Minutes, Central Committee,* 1972, pp. 148–49; *Nairobi Report,* pp. 106, 172–74; *Minutes, Executive Committee,* March 1976, p. 21; *Minutes, Executive Committee,* August 1976, pp. 5–7; *Minutes, Central Committee,* 1976, pp. 12–15; *Minutes, Central Committee,* 1979, pp. 64–65; Executive Committee, September 1979, *Ecumenical Review* 32:80–81; ibid., pp. 325–26, 333; Central Committee, 1980, ibid., p. 435.

56. *The Church and Human Rights,* pp. 42–45, paras. 64–65, 67, 69, in part quoting *Octogesima Adveniens;* p. 48, paras. 75–76; p. 49, para. 78; p. 51, paras. 82–83; pp.59–60, para. 101.

57. *Minutes, Executive Committee,* February 1970, p. 13; *Minutes, Executive Committee,* February 1970, pp. 30–31; *Minutes, Executive Committee,* January 1973, p. 9; *Minutes, Executive Committee,* April 1975, p. 3; *Minutes, Central Committee,* 1974, pp. 40–41; *Minutes, Central Committee,* 1975, pp. 14–15; *Nairobi Report,* pp. 115–18, 162–64, 172–74, 178–79; *Minutes, Executive Committee,* November 1975, p. 3; *Minutes, Central Committee,* 1976, pp. 44–48; *Minutes, Central Committee,* 1977, pp. 35–38; Executive Committee, February 1977, *Ecumenical Review* 29:197; letter of Philip Potter on the request of the Executive Committee to the Ethiopian government, 27 May 1977, *Ecumenical Review* 29:309; *Ecumenical Review* 30:59–64, reporting the CCIA's Helsinki monitoring groups; *Minutes, Central Committee,* 1979, pp. 64, 73–76; Potter's appeal to Iran's Khomeini, Christmas 1979, *Ecumenical Review* 32:192; Central Committee, 1980, ibid., p. 436; *Ecumenical Review* 33:73–75, on the 1980 Soviet trials of Christian "dissidents"; Potter's statements on Palestinian rights, 19 May 1981, ibid., pp. 298–99; Central Committee 1981, ibid., pp. 388, 389.

58. *Minutes, Central Committee,* 1969, p. 22; *Minutes, Central Committee,* 1973, pp. 19–23; *Minutes, Central Committee,* 1975, p. 15; *Nairobi Report,* pp. 117, 172–74, 178–79, 253; *Minutes, Executive Committee,* November 1975, pp. 3–4.

59. *Minutes, Executive Committee,* September 1971, p. 99.

60. *Minutes, Central Committee,* 1967, pp. 51–52, reaffirming Evanston 1954 and Geneva 1966.

61. Statement on apartheid at the World Conference for Action Against Apartheid by Archbishop Girolamo Prigione, Vatican delegate.

62. Ibid. Cf. address of Paul VI to the United Nations Special Committee on Apartheid, 27 May 1974; address of Paul VI to diplomats accredited to the Vatican, 14 January 1978, *Origins* 7:502–3.

63. *Uppsala Report,* p. 241.

64. Ibid., p. 65. The Nairobi Assembly reaffirmed this definition and judgment: *Nairobi Report,* pp. 109–10.

65. Message to the peoples of Africa, 29 October 1967, in Gremillion, ed., p. 422. See also *Octogesima Adveniens* 16; address to diplomats accredited to the Holy See, 14 January 1978, *Origins* 7:502–3; John Paul II, speech to diplomats, Nairobi, 6 May 1980, *Origins* 10:31–32.

66. Address of Pope Paul VI to diplomats accredited to the Holy See, 14 January 1978, *Origins* 7:502–3.

67. *Minutes, Central Committee,* 1967, p. 51; *Minutes, Executive Committee,* January 1969, pp. 15–17; *Minutes, Central Committee,* 1969, pp. 39–40; *Minutes, Executive Committee,* February 1972, pp. 30–31; *Minutes, Central Committee,* 1972, pp. 31–32; *Minutes, Central Committee,* 1973, pp. 199, 201; *Nairobi Report,* pp. 111–13, 119 (a list of trouble spots that omits discrimination against Asians in East Africa, no doubt with an eye to the sensibilities of the host country!), 306; *Minutes, Central Committee,* 1976, pp. 44–48; *Minutes, Central Committee,* 1977, pp. 35–38; Executive Committee, February 1977, *Ecumenical Review* 29:198–99; Executive Committee, February 1978, *Ecumenical Review* 30:166–67; Executive Committee, September 1978, *Ecumenical Review* 31:95; Executive Committee, September 1979, *Ecumenical Review* 32:81; *Minutes, Central Committee,* 1979, pp. 59–61, 73–76; Executive Committee, February 1980, *Ecumenical Review* 32:190–91; message of Philip Potter to the churches of Zimbabwe, 18 April 1980, ibid., pp. 324–25; Central Committee, 1980, ibid., pp. 432–33, 439; Executive Committee, February 1981, *Ecumenical Review* 33:190; Central Committee 1981, ibid., 386–87, 389.

68. *Uppsala Report,* pp. 66, 241; *Minutes, Executive Committee,* January 1969, p. 26; *Minutes, Executive Committee,* February 1974, p. 16; *Minutes, Central Committee,* 1973, pp. 199, 201; *Nairobi Report,* p. 110; and see the examples cited at note 67.

69. *Uppsala Report,* p. 66; *Minutes, Central Committee,* 1971, pp. 56–57, 238; *Nairobi Report,* p. 110.

70. *Minutes, Central Committee,* 1969, pp. 7–9, 27, 271–79; *Uppsala Report,* p. 66; *Minutes, Executive Committee,* August-September 1970, pp. 12–13; *Minutes, Central Committee,* 1971, pp. 55, 238, 241; *Minutes, Executive Committee,* September 1971, pp. 95–96; *Minutes, Executive Committee,* January 1973, pp. 39–40; *Minutes, Central Committee,* 1972, pp. 29–30, 71–72; *Minutes, Central Committee,* 1973, pp. 202–3; *Minutes, Central Committee,* 1974, pp. 36–38; *Nairobi Report,* pp. 118–19; *Minutes, Executive Committee,* November 1975, p. 10; *Minutes, Executive Committee,* August 1976, p. 16; *Minutes, Central Committee,* 1976, pp. 36, 111 (an amendment to add to the grant restrictions "and not for military purposes" was rejected as "unnecessary"); the PCR, defending its grant to the Patriotic Front of Zimbabwe, 11 August 1978, *Ecumenical Review* 30:380–82; Executive Committee, September 1978,

Ecumenical Review 31:94–95; *Minutes, Central Committee,* 1979, pp. 54–60; Central Committee, 1980, *Ecumenical Review* 32:442; ibid., pp. 443–44; Executive Committee, February 1981, *Ecumenical Review* 33:198; *Ecumenical Review* 34:82–83; ibid., pp. 85–86.

71. *Minutes, Executive Committee,* January 1973, p. 19.

72. *Minutes, Executive Committee,* September 1971, p. 93.

73. *Uppsala Report,* p. 64. Cf. *Populorum Progressio* 64, 78; *Minutes, Central Committee,* 1967, p. 116; *Minutes, Central Committee,* 1971, pp. 66–69, 269–76; *The Church and Human Rights,* p. 67, para. 117; p. 68, para. 118; *Church Alert,* no. 18, pp. 18–19.

74. *Uppsala Report,* p. 52. Cf. ibid., pp. 48, 49, 70, 170, 219, 493; *Minutes, Central Committee,* 1972, pp. 145–46, 149–51; *Minutes, Central Committee,* 1974, p. 39; *Nairobi Report,* pp. 165–66, 248, 251; *Ecumenical Review* 30:66; Potter's speech to the U.N. special session on disarmament, 12 June 1978, ibid., pp. 398–99; *Minutes, Central Committee,* 1979, pp. 75–76; Executive Committee, September 1979, *Ecumenical Review* 32:82; Central Committee, 1980, ibid., p. 430; message of Maurice Cardinal Roy as president of Justice and Peace to U Thant on the occasion of the launching of the second U.N. development decade, 19 November 1970, Gremillion, ed., p. 481; *Octogesima Adveniens* 17, 43, 46; *Justice in the World,* Gremillion, ed., pp. 518, 526, 527; Paul VI, World Day of Peace Message, 1 January 1975, ibid., pp. 609–10; address of Archbishop Agostino Casaroli, secretary of the Vatican Council for the Public Affairs of the Church (now Vatican Secretary of State), representing Pope Paul at the U.N. observance of World Day of Peace, New York, 23 January 1978, *Origins* 7:533–34; message of Pope Paul VI to the U.N. General Assembly Special Session on Disarmament, 6 June 1978, delivered by Archbishop Casaroli, *Origins* 8:69–72; John Paul II, address to the U.N. General Assembly, 2 October 1979, *Origins* 9:259; John Paul II, speech before President Carter at the White House, Washington, 6 October 1979, ibid., p. 300; John Paul II, speech to cardinals, 27 December 1979, ibid., pp. 500–502; John Paul II, speech to diplomats, Nairobi, 6 May 1980, *Origins* 10:32; John Paul II, appeal for the Sahel, Ouagadougou, Upper Volta, 10 May 1980, ibid., pp. 45–46; John Paul II, speech at Hiroshima, 25 February 1981, ibid., p. 620; John Paul II, World Day of Peace message, 21 December 1981, *Origins* 11:474.

75. E.g., *Nairobi Report,* pp. 56, 64, 79.

76. *Minutes, Central Committee,* 1967, pp. 44, 116; *Minutes, Executive Committee,* February 1967, p. 15; *Uppsala Report,* pp. 189, 494; *Minutes, Central Committee,* 1969, pp. 68–69; *Minutes, Central Committee,* August-September 1970, p. 17; *Minutes, Central Committee,* 1971, p. 70; *Minutes, Central Committee,* 1972, pp. 28, 152; *Minutes, Executive Committee,* February 1974, pp. 18–19; *Minutes, Central Committee,* 1974, p. 42; *Minutes, Executive Committee,* April 1975, p. 15; *Nairobi Report,* pp. 105, 165–66, 176–77; *Minutes, Executive Com-*

mittee 1976, pp. 25–26; *Minutes, Central Committee*, 1976, p. 43; *Minutes, Central Committee*, 1977, p. 31; *Minutes, Central Committee*, 1979, p. 71; Executive Committee, February 1980, *Ecumenical Review*, 32:189–90.

77. *Minutes, Central Committee*, 1967, pp. 47–48; *Uppsala Report*, p. 47; *Minutes, Central Committee*, 1969, pp. 55, 68, 77–78.

78. *Nairobi Report*, pp. 47, 80, 87.

79. *Justice in the World*, Gremillion, ed., pp. 512, 517–18.

80. John Paul II, speech to youth at Gniezno, Poland, 3 June 1979, *Origins* 9:57–58; John Paul II, address at the monastery of Jasna Gora, 5 June 1979, ibid., p. 71; John Paul II, address to the Executive Council of UNESCO, Paris, 2 June 1980, *Origins* 10:62; John Paul II, homily at Otranto, Italy, 5 October 1980, ibid., p. 274; Vatican report on the visit of Israeli Foreign Minister Yitzhak Shamir to the pope, *Origins* 11:531; John Paul II, address to diplomats accredited to the Vatican, 16 January 1982, ibid., p. 561; John Paul II, address to the diplomatic corps, Lagos, Nigeria, 16 February 1982, ibid., p. 590. On the WCC and Jerusalem, see *Ecumenical Review* 33:78.

81. *Evangelii Nuntiandi* 20; Paul VI, message to the Peoples of Africa, 29 October 1967, Gremillion, ed., pp. 418–21; Paul VI, letter to the Federation of Asian Bishops' Conferences, First General Assembly, Taipei, 21 April 1974, Gremillion, ed., p. 570; *Catechesi Tradendae* 53; John Paul II, message for World Mission Sunday, 21 October 1979, *Origins* 9:174–75; John Paul II, address to Zairean bishops, Kinshasha, 3 May 1980, *Origins* 10:5–6; John Paul II, homily in Nairobi, 7 May 1980, ibid., p. 27; John Paul II, address to bishops of Kenya, Nairobi, 7 May 1980, ibid., p. 29; John Paul II, radio message from Manila to Asian peoples, ibid., p. 612; John Paul II, radio message from Manila to Chinese Christians, ibid., p. 614; John Paul II, letter to all bishops concerning the Chinese church, *Origins* 11:554–55; John Paul II, speech to Nigerian bishops, Lagos, 15 February 1982, ibid., p. 586.

82. E.g., *The Holy See and Disarmament*; statement to the United Nations Disarmament Committee by Msgr. Giovanni Cheli, permanent observer of the Holy See to the United Nations, 12 December 1975, quoting extensively from the documents of Vatican II and papal addresses and encyclicals, pp. 12–16.

83. E.g., *The Holy See and Disarmament*, pp. 10–11.

84. *Minutes, Central Committee*, 1967, pp. 178–79, 48; *Minutes, Executive Committee*, February 1968, p. 24; *Uppsala Report*, pp. 149–58, 170; *Minutes, Executive Committee*, January 1969, p. 16; *Minutes, Executive Committee*, February 1970, pp. 11–12; *Minutes, Central Committee*, 1972, pp. 150, 154; *Minutes, Executive Committee*, 1973, p. 9; *Minutes, Executive Committee*, April 1975, pp. 17–18.

85. *The Holy See and Disarmament*, pp. 1–9; Paul VI, address to the U.N. General Assembly, 4 October 1965, Gremillion, ed., pp. 383–84; Paul VI, World Day of Peace Message, 1 January 1978, *Origins* 7:452; address of Archbishop Casaroli representing Pope Paul at the U.N. ob-

servance of World Day of Peace, New York, 23 January 1978, ibid., pp. 531-34; message of Pope Paul VI to the U.N. General Assembly Special Session on Disarmament, 6 June 1978, delivered by Casaroli, *Origins* 8:69-72; Paul VI, speech opening the fourth Synod of Bishops, 27 September 1974; John Paul II, World Day of Peace Message, 1 January 1979, *Origins* 8:455-60; *Redemptor Hominis* 16; John Paul II, homily at Birkenau (Auschwitz II), 7 June 1979, *Origins* 9:73-74; John Paul II, address to U.N. General Assembly, 2 October 1979, ibid., pp. 261-62; John Paul II, address at the White House, Washington, 6 October 1979, ibid., p. 300; John Paul, speech to the Executive Council of UNESCO, Paris, 2 June 1980, *Origins* 10:64; John Paul II, speech at Hiroshima, 25 February 1981, ibid., p. 620; John Paul II, speech at Castelgondolfo, Italy, *Origins* 11:194; address of the Vatican delegate, Msgr. Mario Peressin, to the International Atomic Energy Agency, Vienna, 22 September 1981, ibid., pp. 266-67; John Paul II, World Day of Peace message, 21 December 1981, ibid., pp. 477-78; message to world leaders from the Pontifical Academy of Sciences, on the direction of John Paul II, ibid., pp. 479-89; *Minutes, Central Committee*, 1967, p. 44; *Uppsala Report*, pp. 124, 132, 140, 180-81; *Minutes, Central Committee*, 1977, p. 31; *Minutes, Central Committee*, 1978, pp. 49-52, 164-66; speech of Philip Potter to the U.N. General Assembly Special Session on Disarmament, 12 June 1978, *Ecumenical Review* 30:398-99; Central Committee, 1980, *Ecumenical Review* 32:434.

86. *Origins* 11:438; text in ibid., pp. 479-80.

87. *The Holy See and Disarmament*, p. 12; *Minutes, Executive Committee*, February 1967, pp. 17-18; *Uppsala Report*, pp. 62-63; *Minutes, Executive Committee*, August-September 1970, pp. 58-59; *Nairobi Report*, pp. 181-82; Executive Committee, February 1980, *Ecumenical Review* 32:189-90; Central Committee, 1980, ibid., p. 434; Central Committee 1981, *Ecumenical Review* 33:383, 384-85.

88. Statement on apartheid by Archbishop Prigione, Vatican delegate. Cf. address of Paul VI to the U.N. Special Committee on Apartheid, 22 May 1974; Paul VI, World Day of Peace Message, 1978, *Origins* 7:452; address of John Paul II . . . at Puebla, I.4; John Paul II to workers in São Paulo, Brazil, 3 July 1980, *Origins* 10:138; John Paul II, address to cardinals and curia, 22 December 1980, ibid., p. 494.

89. *Evangelii Nuntiandi* 36; Paul VI, World Day of Peace message of 1 January 1978, *Origins* 7:449, 451-54; address of Archbishop Casaroli representing Pope Paul at the U.N. observance of World Day of Peace, 23 January 1978, *Origins* 7:533; Paul VI, address to diplomats accredited to the Holy See, ibid., p. 503; *The Church and Human Rights*, p. 38, para. 57 (quoting *Populorum Progressio*), p. 39, para. 59; *Octogesima Adveniens* 26; John Paul II, speech at Drogheda, Ireland, 29 September 1979, *Origins* 9:272-75; John Paul II, World Day of Peace message, 18 December 1979, ibid., p. 458; John Paul II, speech to workers in São Paulo, *Origins* 10:138; John Paul II, speech in Bahia, Brazil, 6 July 1980, ibid., pp. 126-27; John Paul II, speech to poor in Manila, 18 February

1981, ibid., p. 616; John Paul II, speech in Bacolod, Philippines, 20 February 1981, ibid., pp. 618–19.

90. *Minutes, Central Committee*, 1971, p. 55; *Minutes, Executive Committee*, August-September 1970, pp. 12–13.

91. *Uppsala Report*, p. 67.

92. *Minutes, Executive Committee*, February 1972, p. 30.

93. *Minutes, Central Committee*, 1974, pp. 33–35.

94. *Uppsala Report*, pp. 48, 92.

95. *Minutes, Central Committee*, 1971, p. 55.

96. *Minutes, Central Committee*, 1973, pp. 19–23. The text is in *Ecumenical Review* 25:429–46. See also the Program to Combat Racism, justifying its grant to the Patriotic Front of Zimbabwe, *Ecumenical Review* 30:380–82; Executive Committee, September 1979, for a nonviolent solution in Ireland, *Ecumenical Review* 32:76.

97. *Minutes, Central Committee*, 1969, p. 251. Cf. *Uppsala Report*, p. 61.

98. *Justice in the World*, Gremillion, ed., p. 528. See also ibid., pp. 522–23; *Populorum Progressio* 17, 22, 43, 44, 48, 49; intervention of the Vatican delegate, Bishop Edouard Gagnon, at Habitat, the U.N. Conference on Human Settlements, 2 June 1976, *Origins* 6:79–80; John Paul II, address at Puebla, III.4; *Redemptor Hominis* 16; John Paul II in Rio de Janeiro, 2 July 1980, *Origins* 10:123.

99. *Nairobi Report*, p. 128. See also ibid., p. 140; *Uppsala Report*, p. 45; *Minutes, Executive Committee*, February 1974, p. 20.

100. *Minutes, Central Committee*, 1969, pp. 21–22. See also *Uppsala Report*, pp. 48ff.; *Nairobi Report*, p. 306; Central Committee 1981, *Ecumenical Review* 33:384; *Octogesima Adveniens* 43; Message of Cardinal Roy, president of Justice and Peace, to U Thant, 19 November 1970, Gremillion, ed., pp. 480–81; *Justice in the World*, ibid., pp. 516–17; John Paul II, message for World Mission Sunday, 21 October 1979, *Origins* 9:175–76; John Paul II, address to the U.N. General Assembly, 2 October 1979, ibid., p. 264; John Paul II, speech to diplomats, Nairobi, 6 May 1980, *Origins* 10:32; John Paul II, speech in Rio de Janeiro, 2 July 1980, ibid., p. 124; John Paul II, radio message from Manila to Asian peoples, 21 February 1981, ibid., pp. 611–12; John Paul II, speech at Hiroshima, 25 February 1981, ibid., pp. 622–23.

101. *Populorum Progressio* 5, 13, 17, 22, 42, 43, 44, 48, 49, 51, 52, 53, 57–61, 84; *Justice in the World*, Gremillion, ed., pp. 527–28; message of Cardinal Roy to U Thant, 19 November 1970, ibid., pp. 477–84; Paul VI, message to the Peoples of Africa, 29 October 1967, ibid., pp. 423–24; *The Church and Human Rights*, p. 26, para. 38, no. 14, p. 66, para. 113; intervention of the Vatican delegate, Bishop Gagnon, at Habitat, 2 June 1976, *Origins* 6:79; Roger Heckel, secretary of Justice and Peace, *Self-Reliance*, Vatican City, 1978, summarizing recent Catholic teaching, passim; John Paul II, speech to diplomats, Nairobi, 6 May 1980, *Origins* 10:31; John Paul II, speech to workers, São Paulo, 3 July 1980, ibid., pp. 138–39; *Laborem Exercens* 17, 21; John Paul II, address to diplomats

accredited to the Vatican, 16 January 1982, *Origins* 11:563; *Uppsala Report*, pp. 46, 48, 53, 68; *Minutes, Executive Committee*, February 1970, p. 77; Denys Munby, ed., *World Development, Challenge to the Churches*, Corpus Books, Washington and Cleveland, 1969, passim (report of the Sodepax conference at Beirut, 21–27 April 1968); *Minutes, Central Committee*, 1971, p. 64; *Minutes, Central Committee*, 1972, pp. 26–27, 146, 272–74; *Minutes, Central Committee*, 1974, pp. 22–23; *Nairobi Report*, pp. 122–24, 248; *Minutes, Central Committee*, 1976, p. 34; *Minutes, Central Committee*, 1977, pp. 29–30, 43–45; *Minutes, Central Committee*, 1979, pp. 68–70; Central Committee, 1981, *Ecumenical Review* 33:383.

102. "Human Development and Christian Salvation," International Theological Commission (advisory to pope), September 1977, *Origins* 7:305, 307–13.

103. Paul VI, address to the World Food Conference, Rome, 9 November 1974, Gremillion, ed., p. 602; Justice and Peace, *The Universal Purpose of Created Things* (Vatican City, 1977), passim; *Populorum Progressio* 22, 48, 49; *Uppsala Report*, pp. 50–51; *Nairobi Report*, p. 127; Central Committee, 1980, *Ecumenical Review* 32:435, 437–39.

104. *The Universal Purpose of Created Things; Octogesima Adveniens* 14, 43–44; *Justice in the World*, Gremillion, ed., pp. 515–16; John Paul II at Puebla, III.4; John Paul II, speech to Indian peasants in Cuilapan, Mexico, 29 January 1979, *Origins* 8:544; John Paul II, speech to workers in Guadalajara, 30 January 1979, ibid., pp. 557–58; John Paul II, speech to Brazilian bishops, Fortaleza, 10 July 1980, *Origins* 10:136; John Paul II, address in Bacolod, Philippines, 20 February 1981, ibid., pp. 618–19; *Laborem Exercens* 2, 7, 8, 11–15, 18, 19, 20; John Paul II, homily at Lagos Cathedral, Nigeria, 16 February 1982, *Origins* 11:596; *Uppsala Report*, pp. 51, 51; *Minutes, Central Committee*, 1967, p. 47; *Minutes, Central Committee*, 1977, pp. 32–33, 110–13; *Nairobi Report*, p. 131.

105. *Uppsala Report*, p. 88; cf. p. 54.

106. *Populorum Progressio*, 25; cf. 22.

107. John Paul II, address to the Pontifical Academy of Sciences, 10 November 1979, *Origins* 9:390; John Paul II, speech to the Executive Council of UNESCO, Paris, 2 June 1980, *Origins* 10:63–64; John Paul II, address to German scholars and students in Cologne Cathedral, 15 November 1980, ibid., pp. 395–98; letter from Cardinal Casaroli, Vatican secretary of state, "on behalf of the Holy Father," to the rector of the Catholic Institute of Paris on the centenary of Teilhard's birth, *Origins* 11:113, 115; John Paul II, speech to scientists at Castelgondolfo, Italy, 3 October 1981, *Origins* 11:279; John Paul II to scholars at the University of Ibadan, Nigeria, 15 February 1982, ibid., p. 595.

108. *Octogesima Adveniens* 21, 38–40; *Redemptor Hominis* 15, 16; John Paul II, speech in Nowy Tarz, Poland, 8 June 1979, *Origins* 9:75; John Paul II, homily near Des Moines, Iowa, 4 October 1979, ibid., pp. 293–94; John Paul II, speech at Kisangani, Zaire, 6 May 1980, *Origins* 10:23; *Laborem Exercens*, warnings scattered throughout the generally

positive encyclical; *Minutes, Central Committee*, 1971, p. 75; *Nairobi Report*, pp. 78, 88, 125–29, 134–35.

109. See the report of the conference at Massachusetts Institute of Technology, Cambridge, Mass., 1979, *Faith and Science in an Unjust World: Report of the W.C.C. Conference on Faith, Science, and the Future*, 2 vols., ed. Paul Abrecht (Geneva: World Council of Churches, 1980). A study conference, its findings are not formal declarations of the WCC. See also Paul VI, address to the U.N. General Assembly, 4 October 1965, Gremillion, ed., p. 386; John Paul II, speech to diplomats, Nairobi, 6 May 1980, *Origins* 10:32; John Paul II, appeal for the Sahel, Ouagadougou, Upper Volta, 10 May 1980, ibid., p. 45; John Paul II to workers in São Paulo, 3 July 1980, ibid., p. 139; *Dives in Misericordia* 2, 10; John Paul II, address at the U.N. University, Hiroshima, 25 February 1981, *Origins* 10:621–23; *Laborem Exercens* 1, 4, 5, 9, 10, 25, 26, and passim.

110. *Minutes, Executive Committee*, February 1967, p. 17; *Minutes, Central Committee*, 1976, pp. 38, 109–10 (includes the WCC submission to the International Atomic Energy Agency, Salzburg, 9 May 1977, also in *Ecumenical Review* 29:315); *Minutes, Central Committee*, 1977, pp. 18–21; *Nairobi Report*, pp. 125–29, 138–39; *Minutes, Central Committee*, 1979, p. 42; Central Committee 1980, *Ecumenical Review* 32:441–42; statement of Msgr. Mario Peressin, Vatican observer to the U.N. Organization for Industrial Development, made to the International Atomic Energy Agency, Vienna, 24 September 1980, *Origins* 10:460–63.

111. *Minutes, Central Committee*, 1967, p. 47; *Uppsala Report*, p. 50. Cf. *Minutes, Central Committee*, 1971, p. 75; *Uppsala Report*, p. 92; *Nairobi Report*, pp. 108, 124, 137, 309.

112. John Paul II, address before the president of Brazil, Brasilia, 30 June 1980, *Origins* 10:128.

113. Statement of Msgr. James McHugh, Vatican representative to the U.N. Population Commission meeting, 26 January–4 February 1981, *Origins* 10:564.

114. Address to the U.N. General Assembly, 4 October 1965, Gremillion, ed., p. 385.

115. Paul VI, address to the World Food Conference, Rome, 9 November 1974, Gremillion, ed., p. 604.

116. John Paul II, homily on Washington Mall, 7 October 1979, *Origins* 9:279.

117. John Paul II, *Familiaris Consortio* (Apostolic Exhortation on the Family), 22 November 1981, para. 30.

118. *Humanae Vitae* 14.

119. *Humanae Vitae* 16; John Paul II, address to cardinals and curia, 22 December 1980, *Origins* 10:495; John Paul II, address to the Congress for the Family of Africa and Europe, 15 January 1981, *Origins* 10:527–28; statement by Msgr. James McHugh for the Holy See at a meeting of the Steering Committee on Population of the Council of Europe, July 1981, *Origins* 11:114; *Familiaris Consortio* 6, 28, 32.

120. In addition to the sources for the quotations (notes 112–19 above), see also *The Church and Human Rights*, p. 25 para. 38, no. 5; *Populorum Progressio* 37; *Humanae Vitae* 11–17, 21, 23–25 and passim; *Octogesima Adveniens* 8, 18; *Justice in the World*, Gremillion, ed., pp. 517–19; message of Cardinal Roy to U Thant, 19 November 1970, 16 iv, ibid., pp. 482–83; intervention by Bishop Edouard Gagnon, head of the Holy See's delegation to the U.N. Population Conference, Bucharest, 30 August 1974, ibid., pp. 589–91; statement of the Vatican Congregation for the Doctrine of the Faith, on sterilization, 13 March 1975, *Origins* 6:35, 37; the "Declaration on Sexual Ethics" of the Congregation for the Doctrine of the Faith, 15 January 1976, *Origins* 5:485, 487–94; Paul VI, address to the College of Cardinals, 23 June 1978, *Origins* 8:110; Paul VI, homily on themes of his pontificate, 29 June 1978, ibid., p. 120; Paul VI, remarks to the executive director of UNICEF, 28 June 1978, ibid., p. 121; remarks of Msgr. James McHugh on behalf of the Holy See to the U.N. Population Commission, 30 January 1979, ibid., p. 572; letter of Cardinal Jean Villot, Vatican secretary of state, to the International Federation for Family Life Promotion, June 1977, speaking for Paul VI, *Origins* 7:125; preliminary Vatican paper for the 1980 bishops' synod on "the role of the family," *Origins* 9:116–17, 121, and passim; John Paul II, address to U.S. bishops, Chicago, 5 October 1979, ibid., p. 289; John Paul II, homily in County Limerick, Ireland, 1 October 1979, ibid., p. 325; John Paul II, address at Puebla, III.5, IV.1; John Paul II to bishops of Kenya, Nairobi, 7 May 1980, *Origins* 10:29; John Paul II to cardinals and curia, 28 June 1980, ibid., p. 173; John Paul II, message to the Synod of Bishops, September-October 1980, 25 October 1980, ibid., pp. 323, 328–29; John Paul II, closing homily to the Synod of Bishops, 25 October 1980, ibid., pp. 327–28; statement of Msgr. James McHugh, Vatican representative, to the U.N. Population Commission, 26 January–4 February 1981, ibid., pp. 561, 563–64; John Paul II, speech before President Ferdinand Marcos of the Philippines, 17 February 1981, ibid., p. 591; John Paul II, speech in Cebu, Philippines, 19 February 1981, ibid., pp. 636–37; *Familiaris Consortio* 11, 16, 29, 32, 33, 34, 35, 37, 72; John Paul II, speech to Nigerian bishops, Lagos, 15 February 1982, *Origins* 11:587.

121. *Uppsala Report*, pp. 50, 68, 92; *Minutes, Central Committee*, 1973, p. 71; *Nairobi Report*, p. 108; *World Development, Challenge to the Churches*, p. 5, a joint WCC/Holy See project that was bound to be ambiguous on contraception.

122. For a bare sample of statements against abortion in recent pronouncements, see *Octogesima Adveniens* 18; *Justice in the World*, Gremillion, ed., p. 519; Declaration on Abortion, Vatican Congregation for the Doctrine of the Faith, 18 November 1974, *Origins* 4:385, 387–92; remarks of Msgr. James McHugh to the U.N. Population Commission, *Origins* 8:572; John Paul II on the Washington Mall, *Origins* 9:279; John Paul II, homily in County Limerick, Ireland, 1 October 1979, ibid., p. 325; message of the 1980 Bishops' Synod, *Origins* 10:328–29; John Paul

II in Cebu, Philippines, ibid., p. 636; John Paul II, Easter message, 19 April 1981, ibid., p. 736 (a month before the Italian abortion referendum); Vatican statement on the U.N. International Year of Disabled Persons, ibid., pp. 747–50; John Paul II, Sunday remarks from the balcony of St. Peter's, a week before the abortion referendum, 10 May 1981, *Origins* 11:2; John Paul II, Motu proprio of 9 May 1981 announcing the new Pontifical Council for the Family, ibid., pp. 63–64; *Familiaris Consortio* 6; John Paul II, speech to Nigerian bishops, Lagos, 15 February 1982, ibid. p. 587.

123. Declaration of the Vatican Congregation for the Doctrine of the Faith, 26 June 1980, *Origins* 10:154–57; John Paul II to Italian doctors, 27 October 1980, ibid., pp. 351–52, a statement possibly working at cross-purposes with his cultivation of scientists and celebration of technology.

124. *Minutes, Central Committee*, 1977, p. 51. See also *Uppsala Report*, pp. 64, 92, 250; *Minutes, Central Committee*, 1971, p. 32; *Nairobi Report*, pp. 105, 107, 113; *Minutes, Central Committee*, 1979, pp. 80–82.

125. *Uppsala Report*, p. 250; *Minutes, Central Committee*, 1974, pp. 46–47, 49; *Minutes, Executive Committee*, April 1975, pp. 28–29, 30–32; *Nairobi Report*, pp. 62, 109, 114, 309; *Minutes, Executive Committee*, March 1976, p. 22; Central Committee 1981, *Ecumenical Review* 33:390.

126. *Uppsala Report*, pp. 92–94; *Nairobi Report*, pp. 109, 115, 310.

127. *The Church and Human Rights*, p. 25 para. 38, no. 7 and note 56, p. 65, para. 111; *Humanae Vitae* 9; *Octogesima Adveniens* 13, 18; *Evangelii Nuntiandi* 29; Paul VI, message to the peoples of Africa, 29 October 1967, Gremillion, ed., pp. 418–21, 424–25; Paul VI, World Day of Peace Message, 1 January 1975, ibid., p. 611; John Paul II to the National Congress of Italian Domestic Workers, 29 April 1979, quoting Pius XII with approval, *Origins* 9:32; message of the Synod of Bishops, September-October 1980, whose theme was family life, *Origins* 10:325; John Paul II to closing session of the synod, ibid., p. 328; *Laborem Exercens* 9, 19; *Familiaris Consortio* 22–25.

128. "Can Women Be Priests?" Report of the Pontifical Biblical Commission, intended for the Vatican Congregation on Doctrine but made public by press leak in June 1976, *Origins* 6:95–96; *The Church and Human Rights*, p. 25, note 56; Declaration on the Admission of Women to the Ministerial Priesthood, by the Vatican Congregation for the Doctrine of the Faith, *Origins* 6:517, 519–24; joint communiqué on the Roman Catholic Church-Russian Orthodox Church meeting, 17 March 1980, *Origins* 9:704–5.

129. *Familiaris Consortio* 11, 13, 19, 20, 40, 45, 46, 78, 80–84.

130. "Deepening Communion: An Account of the Current Work of the Joint Working Group," *Ecumenical Review* 32:182–83; *Ecumenical Review* 34:84.

INDEX

abortion, 21, 37, 70
Action for Food Production (AF-PRO), 32, 60
action-reflection model of ethics, 11, 13
Afghanistan, 21, 49
Africa, 45, 51, 67. *See also* South Africa, southern Africa; references to individual nations
agriculture, 59, 60, 62, 63, 65
Albania, 21
America. *See* United States
Amin, Idi, 21, 41
Anglican Church (Church of England), 5, 71
Angola, 45, 49
Argentina, 21, 42
arms race. *See* disarmament; nuclear weapons; war
Australia, 44
authority. *See* Holy See, authority of; World Council of Churches, authority of
Bantustans. *See* South Africa
Beirut conference on development, 1968 (Sodepax), 60
Biafra. *See* Nigeria
Bible, use of, 11-13, 19
birth control. *See* contraception
Blake, Eugene Carson (General Secretary of WCC), 19, 53
Bolivia, 42

Brazil, 28, 43
Bucharest population conference, 1974 (U.N.), 29
Burma, 42
Canterbury, Archbishop of, 5
capitalism, 61
capital punishment, 40
Caritas Internationalis (Roman Catholic Church), 60
Carter, President Jimmy, 22
celibacy, 16, 33, 68
Central Committee of the World Council of Churches, 10, 39, 40, 42, 57, 64, 75
Chile, 21, 28, 42
China, 54
Chinese "Patriotic" Catholic Church, 29
Christian Medical Commission (CMC), 31-32
church, function of, 5-6, 19. *See also* Roman Catholic Church, church, conception of
Church Alert (journal of Sodepax), 30
Church and Society, Department of (WCC), 32
Churches' Commission on International Affairs (CCIA), 9-10, 26, 27, 29, 32, 43, 53
Church of England (Anglican Church), 5, 71

97

matters, 12, 18, 21; on nationalism, 47-48, 50-52; on the ordination of women, 73-74; on political participation, 19, 20, 84n.31; on population growth, 64-69; on racism, 43-44, 46-47; relation to national and local churches, 25, 26, 33, 34, 51, 77-78; as state, 27-30; on violence, revolution, war, and pacificism, 52-58

housing, right to, 40, 65, 74
Humanae Vitae, 68-69
human rights, 36-43, 48, 58, 76, 78
ideology, effect of, 13-14, 55, 60
independence. *See* self-determination

India, 42, 44, 51
individualism and community, 37-39
internationalism. *See* nationalism
investment policy, 45-47
Iran, 21, 42
Iraq, 21, 29, 42
Ireland, Northern Ireland, 21, 41, 50, 56
Israel, 21, 49, 51
Italy, 14, 21, 28, 34
Japan, 44
Jerusalem, 51
Jesuits, 5
John Paul II (pope): on abstaining from politics, 19; on the Church, nature of, 16; on ecumenism and Christian unity, 3-5, 7; on El Salvador and Guatemala, 22; on Iran, request to Khomeini, 21; on Israel and Jerusalem, 51; on Marxism, 14; on medical ethics, 70; on national identity, 50-51; on nuclear war, 54; on Poland, 22-23,

41, 51; on the poor and oppressed, 28; on population growth and birth control, 67; on priests and nuns, 15-16, 19-20, 84n.31; on science and technology, 62, 96n.123; visit to England of, 5; visit to Geneva of, 6

Joint Consultative Group on Social Thought and Action (JCG), ix, 78

Joint Working Group of the Roman Catholic Church and the World Council of Churches, vii-ix, 1-3, 6, 47, 78

justice, 17, 20, 37, 46, 47, 55-61, 63

Justice and Peace, Pontifical Commission 1, 7, 20, 27, 30, 32, 34, 47, 47

Kane, Sr. Theresa, 83n.26
Khomeini, Ayatollah Ruhollah, 21
Kingdom of God, 15-17, 60
Korea, 42
Küng, Hans, 4
labor unions, 61
laity, 16, 19-20, 33-34, 69
land, use of. *See* agriculture
Latin America, 11, 32, 41, 42
Law of the Sea Treaty, 61
League of Nations, 49
Lefèbvre affair, 34
liberation, liberation movements, liberation theology, 14-17, 33, 34, 46, 55-59, 70
Life and Work, Universal Christian Council on, 7, 49
Luwum, Archbishop Janani, 41
magisterium. *See* Holy See, authority of
Marcos, President Ferdinand, 21, 41
marriage, 4, 16, 37, 71, 74-75

098889